Twenty-First Century

TEACHING GUIDE FOR INDIAN SCHOOLS

Computer Science 2

Sharmistha Baral brings over 30 years of experience in teaching Computer Science, Computer Studies, Computer Applications and ICT across diverse curricula including ICSE, IGCSE (O and A Levels) and the IB Diploma Programme. Her experience extends to teaching disabled students under the National Institute of Open Schooling (NIOS) curriculum, fostering inclusivity and sensitivity in her classrooms. She has also contributed to innovation in education by mentoring Atal Tinkering Lab incharges in implementing design thinking within the ATL curriculum. As the Computer Science Department Head, she has mentored Computer teachers and guided the teachers of other discipline in integrating ICT effectively into teaching and learning.

Twenty-First Century

TEACHING GUIDE FOR INDIAN SCHOOLS

Computer Science 2

Sharmistha Baral

For Classes 6–8

hachette INDIA

First published in paperback in 2025 by Hachette India
(Registered name: Hachette Book Publishing India Pvt. Ltd)
An Hachette UK company
www.hachetteindia.com

1

All QR codes included in the book lead to video links which belong to the respective channels/video platforms that have posted them. Their availability is subject to the period till the respective channels/video platforms continue to feature them.

All content and facts within the book have been updated and verified to the best extent possible. Any inadvertent omissions brought to our attention in writing will be remedied in future editions.

Subsequent edition/reprint specifications may be subject to change, including but not limited to cover or inside finishes, paper, text colour and/or colour sections.

ISBN 978-93-5731-347-6

Hachette Book Publishing India Pvt. Ltd
4th & 5th Floors, Corporate Centre
Plot No. 94, Sector 44, Gurugram – 122003, India

Typeset by Manmohan Kumar, Delhi

MIX
Paper | Supporting responsible forestry
FSC® C010615
www.fsc.org

Printed and bound in India
by Thomson Press India Ltd.

Contents

Preface

Teaching computer science in the middle school years (grades 6 to 8) is both a challenge and an opportunity. Students at this stage stand at the cusp of childhood curiosity and adolescent reasoning. They are eager to explore, question and create – but they also demand learning that is meaningful, engaging and connected to their world.

This book has been designed as a practical guide for teachers to align classroom teaching with the **National Education Policy (NEP 2020)** and its emphasis on **twenty-first century skills** – critical thinking, creativity, collaboration and communication. It also takes inspiration from global best practices, blending traditional foundations with innovative and hands-on strategies.

The chapters move beyond rote memorization and textbook-driven instruction to showcase how computer science can be taught through **constructivist**, **experiential**, **collaborative and inquiry-based pedagogies**. From role play, flipped classrooms and peer assessments to interdisciplinary projects, storytelling, gamification and project-based learning, each approach has been contextualized with ready-to-use lesson plans, activities and assessment rubrics.

Teachers will also find strategies to integrate digital tools and active learning techniques into their classrooms. Every example – whether it is teaching algorithms through comic strips, number systems through role play or cyber safety through storytelling – is rooted in real classroom experiences. These pedagogies are not theoretical abstractions, but tried and tested methods that have ignited joy and curiosity among middle school learners.

Importantly, this book recognizes the diversity of learners in every classroom. Techniques such as **differentiation**, **multiple intelligence approaches and scaffolding** have been woven in to ensure that students of varied abilities remain engaged, supported and empowered.

It is my hope that this book serves not only as a teaching manual but also as a companion that inspires teachers to experiment, adapt and innovate. Technology changes rapidly, but the role of a teacher as a mentor, facilitator and guide remains timeless. By embracing these strategies, teachers can create classrooms that are inclusive, dynamic and future-ready – spaces where students do not just learn about computers, but learn **with** computers to solve problems, imagine possibilities and build better futures.

Happy Reading!

Chapter 1

Evolution of School Education
Through the Eyes of an Adaptive Teacher

Imagine we are a group of teachers, standing in front of a time machine, and our mission is to understand the past hundred years of evolution in the Indian education system. The time machine, aptly named Garuda, is waiting for us… Try to visualize this: we have boarded Garuda, fastened our seat belts, put on our headphones and are waiting for the adventure to begin. The inside of Garuda is just out of a sci-fi movie. After we are all seated and comfortable, the door closes automatically, the time machine, gives a jerk and begins to ascend. Garuda runs completely on an autopilot system, right from take-off to landing. It starts flying at the speed of light, and everything around us becomes a blur!

Our virtual guide, Apala's metallic voice, informs us briefly about Garuda's safety features with a corresponding

Time Machine Garuda, created with Canva.AI

demonstration visible on the monitor in front of our seats. She goes on to explain the objectives of this trip. 'The Indian education system has been one of the greatest since ancient times,' she continues. 'We are going to begin with a brief introduction to the ancient education system, followed by the medieval education system. Garuda will give us a bird's-eye view of some of the famous educational institutes and cities of the ancient and medieval times.'

Apala then informs us, 'The ancient system focused on the all-around development of a student by providing holistic education. That included not only academics but also physical, emotional, intellectual as well as the spiritual growth of a child. Children were also made aware of the rich cultural and philosophical background of India. The *gurukul* system of education was prevalent during this time, where the students came to the guru's house and stayed there to learn. A deep bond developed between the guru and the disciple.' It is fascinating how the knowledge was transmitted orally and how the students remembered everything verbatim.

Garuda has now visibly slowed down and lost altitude. We are informed that we are flying over Takshashila or Taxila, one of the most famous centres of higher education

Bird's Eye View of Ancient Taxila, created with Canva.AI

in the religious teachings of Gautam Buddha. Students from all over the country, as well as abroad, came here to receive an education. We look down to see the famous university of Taxila as it was.

Apala announces, 'Please put on the Virtual Reality (VR) headset available in the seat pocket in front of you. I will now introduce you to one of the star students of Taxila, followed by other important people of ancient times.' We can hear excited murmurs around us. An AI-powered VR system starts working. We can see Chanakya, also known as Kautilya, walking down the aisle. Chanakya, the author of *Arthashastra* and a great political mastermind, needs no introduction. He talks about the influence of Taxila in moulding him. I ask him to tell us about his importance in Chandragupta Maurya's court. He smiles and looks to his right. We are astounded to find King Chandragupta standing next to him. Together, they briefly discuss their achievements. We also get to interact with Panini, the revered Sanskrit scholar, and Jivaka, the famous physician of Gautama Buddha!

Meeting Chanakya, Chandragupta, Panini and Jivaka via VR

We are now flying over Delhi, Agra, Jaunpur and Bidar, the important places of learning during the mediaeval period. Apala tells us how the education system changed during this period, with the focus being on the propagation of Islam and the spreading of knowledge. Many *maktabs* for primary education, as well as madrasas for higher education, were established by the rulers in the cities over which we are flying. Although the *gurukul* system was not followed, the teacher–student bond was very strong at that time. The main teaching methodology was still oral. However, Emperor Akbar encouraged both reading and writing, and we interact with him as well.

All of us are awestruck. Suddenly, Apala's voice tells us that we have reached the end of our journey. It seems to me as if the experience was a part of my dream.

Coming back to the present, not so long ago, a teacher in the classroom would employ traditional teaching methods such as textbooks, lectures, a chalkboard, more lectures and then written exams. The main objective was to transfer knowledge through one-way communication. The students were considered passive consumers of facts. Rote learning was encouraged, and the students with good retention power would usually excel. A lack of teaching aids and resources made teaching challenging at that time.

However, some teachers would think differently, break the barriers and come out with innovative and engaging methods of teaching, which would make learning a joyful experience among the students. They would retain the knowledge thus inseminated throughout their lives.

During my initial years as a teacher, I would teach geography and computer science. Before teaching about rocks and minerals for the first time to Grade 8, I collected samples from the Geological Survey of India, Kolkata, as well as from the places I visited. In the absence of the internet, I would take photographs of rock formations in their beds and various landforms. I also collected more from my friends and arranged class exhibitions with all the materials. My students were so excited to see, with their own eyes, what they had learnt in class. Many of them would later bring back rocks and photographs of landforms from their family trips to show me.

The concept of school education has changed gradually over time. With the advent of globalization and technology in the field of education, there has been a major paradigm shift in classroom dynamics. Classroom transactions have become bidirectional rather than unidirectional. The teachers and the students work together to gather knowledge by honing the 4Cs of twenty-first century learning skills – communication, collaboration, critical thinking and creativity. The role of a teacher is more of a facilitator or mentor. The modern teacher must understand student psychology, acknowledge the presence of multiple intelligences in the classroom and create or modify the curriculum according to learner profiles. They have to inspire learners and nurture healthy curiosity among them to create meaningful learning experiences in the class. A successful teacher would also research abundantly, learn and implement learning theories and pedagogies relevant to their subjects during classroom transactions. The changed scenario has forced the conventional teachers to come out of their comfort zone and learn to quickly adapt to stay relevant.

Chapter 2

A Snapshot of NEP 2020 and NCF-SE 2023

The National Education Policy (NEP) 2020 envisions a massive transformation in education through 'an education system rooted in Indian ethos that contributes directly to transforming India, that is Bharat, sustainably into an equitable and vibrant knowledge society, by providing high-quality education to all, thereby making India a global knowledge superpower'. The NEP 2020 is founded on the five guiding pillars of access, equity, quality, affordability and accountability. It will prepare our youth to meet the diverse national and global challenges of the present and the future.

NEP 2020 has proposed the inclusion of social and emotional skills along with cognitive skills of numeracy and literacy, and higher-order skills of critical thinking and problem solving. It has recommended a '5+3+3+4' schooling system to cater to the needs of 3- to 18-year-olds, restructuring of curriculum framework, revision of assessment system, introduction to technology-supported education, effective pedagogy and teachers' training to implement the policy, to mention a few.

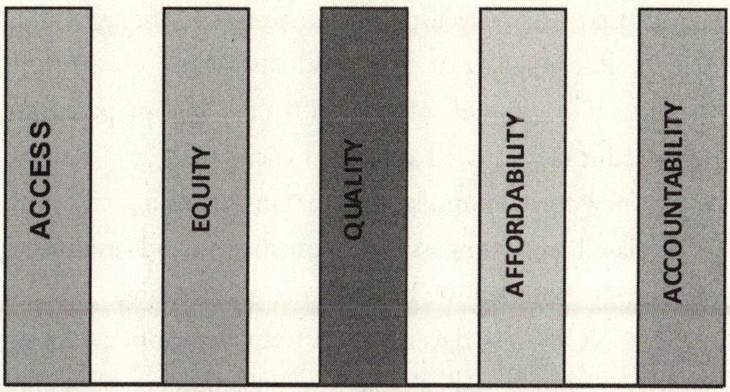

The Five Guiding Pillars of NEP 2020

The National Curriculum Framework for School Education (NCF-SE) 2023 has been designed meticulously by the National Steering Committee (NCF) to implement the changes in school curricula as proposed in NEP 2020 for transforming school education in India.

The content of the NCF has been designed in a manner that all the stakeholders – students, teachers, school administrators, curriculum developers, examinations boards, parents and community members get a fair understanding of the vision of NCF and their role to make this vision a reality.

The NCF's vision is to develop a robust, aspirational and practically implementable NCF, as well as SCFs (State Curriculum Frameworks) that will ensure that all students, irrespective of their circumstances, receive the best possible education, with complete support from the system.

The goal of the new curricula is to foster a school education system that builds well-rounded, healthy, compassionate, caring, ethical and creative individuals, who possess sound character and rational such that they are well-prepared for higher education as well as gainful vocation.

The new curriculum also aims to transform our society into an unbiased, fair, compassionate, prosperous and sustainable one, firmly rooted in the Indian ethos and culture.

The NCF has developed a clear set of 'Learning Standards' which will aid all the stakeholders of school

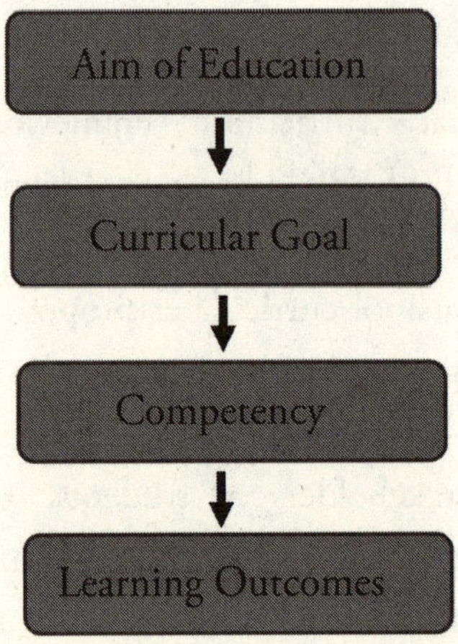

Four Levels of Learning Standards

education to understand which knowledge, capacities, values and dispositions are valuable to develop an aligned and integrated curriculum. The Learning Standards follow definite steps, from the broader Aims of Education to more specific Learning Outcomes.

Keeping in mind the aims and goals of NEP 2020 and NCF-SE 2023, an effort has been made in this book to introduce some best teaching practices, learning theories and pedagogies in action which are best suited to teach computer science and computer studies at the middle-school level.

Chapter 3

Twenty-First Century Learning

The two buzzwords of twenty-first century learning are **HOTS** and **4Cs**. HOTS (Higher Order Thinking Skills) refer to the top three cognitive skills of the modified Bloom's Taxonomy: Analysing, Evaluating and Creating. The 4Cs, communication, collaboration, creativity and critical thinking, are essential twenty-first century skills which are mandatory to help students become successful global citizens, adaptable to any adverse situations in life. HOTS and 4Cs

Bloom's Taxonomy

The taxonomy designed by Benjamin Bloom and others in 1956 defines educational goals in the form of a six-level skills pyramid. This was slightly modified in 2001 to incorporate verbs instead of nouns, ranging from lower-order skills like remembering and understanding to higher-order skills like evaluating and creating.

closely align with each other to foster deeper learning and problem-solving capabilities among the students.

HOTS and 4Cs can be implemented in the classrooms through Inquiry-Based Learning (IBL), Project-Based Learning (PBL), Interdisciplinary Learning and Simulation, as well as Gamification. Each has been discussed in Chapter 4.

Using AR, VR and AI in Classrooms

Augmented Reality (AR) and Virtual Reality (VR) are revolutionizing classroom education by making learning more engaging, immersive and interactive. AR-based programming tutorials, interactive coding books and AR

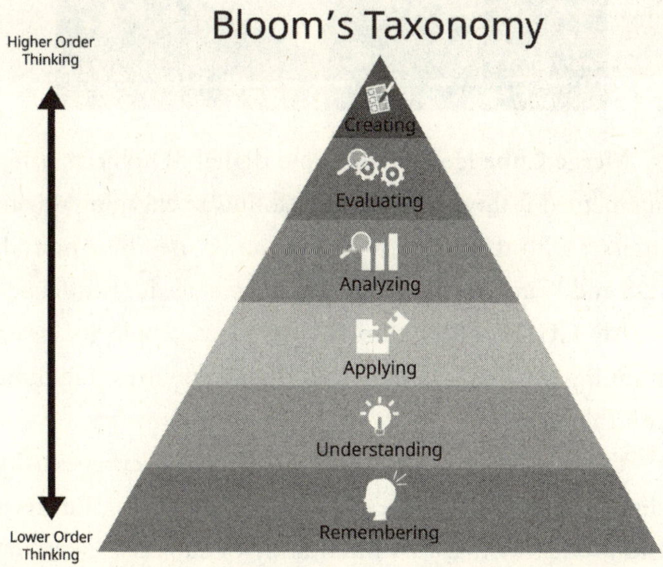

circuit simulation can make learning more interesting without much hassle.

For example, **UNITY** is a popular platform for creating AR and VR content, video games and animations. There is a course for beginners that lets one go through a series of guided tutorials and project work. The course offers certification from UNITY as well. The link: https://learn.unity.com/pathway/junior-programmer

Merge Cube lets the user hold digital 3D objects using augmented reality technology, enabling an engaging way to interact with the digital world. It can be used on Android, iOS and Windows. The link: https://mergeedu. com/cube

AR CODE offers tutorials to allow people to create stunning AR and 3D models. The link: https://ar-code.com/blog/ar-tutorials

VR can be used in virtual coding labs, cybersecurity simulations and VR-based networking labs. **Edutech India** offers virtual labs in an array of subjects, including programming and coding, as well as AI for classes K-12. The link is: https://edutechindia.com/virtual-lab-k12

Google has developed **Blocks**, a VR app for the HTC VIVE and Oculus Rift. It can easily create beautiful 3D objects.

Despite several obstacles like the high cost of VR equipment, insufficient training and limited content, we can find less expensive alternatives like Google Cardboard, online VR platforms, as well as web-based training and VR platforms for the teachers.

The following QR code will take you to a blog which discusses fun AR applications for teachers to use in class.

Fun Apps For Teachers

Being a Twenty-First Century Teacher

The twenty-first century has marked the beginning of a Volatile, Uncertain, Complex and Ambiguous (VUCA) world. Teachers need to prepare themselves to help students face uncertainty by being adaptive and by embracing new technologies and methodologies in education. The role of a teacher now is that of a facilitator rather than an instructor. The students play an equal part in the process of learning, thanks to technology.

To prepare the students as successful global citizens, a teacher must inculcate among the students the 4Cs of twenty-first century skills. Moreover, teachers themselves must hone these skills so they can encourage their students.

The Teacher as a Communicator

Communicating effectively with all the stakeholders is the key to success.

It is essential to make our expectations for the class clear at the beginning of the academic year.

For instance, we may need to occasionally change the class's seating plan to conduct planned activities. It is mandatory to brainstorm about our plans with the class teacher and the subject teachers whose classes may be affected by this arrangement. Necessary modifications to our plans must be made with everyone's cognizance.

The approved seating plans must be communicated to the class in advance to avoid confusion and lessen the time required to arrange the seats before and after the class.

At times, we may want to conduct activities involving interaction with a resource person, a study tour or an inter-class debate, which would require: 1) More time than our usual class time, 2) Might require the involvement of the students of other classes and teachers or 3) Liaison with external agencies. Prior permission from the school administrators and a foolproof plan with the concerned teachers must be made well in advance to make the programme a success.

It is mandatory to use all approved channels of communication to inform the parents about their child's progress.

The Teacher as a Collaborator

Collaboration creates an environment of trust among colleagues, opens one's mind to new ideas and boosts personal growth from positive feedback received from the community. Cross-curricular collaboration develops greater fellowship among the teachers. The students appreciate the interconnection between subjects and develop critical thinking and collaboration skills. To collaborate successfully, a lot of support is required from the administration and colleagues.

A great way to collaborate is to incorporate interdisciplinary projects as a part of the annual lesson plan. To chart out effective cross-curricular activities, we need to brainstorm with the concerned subject teachers to design a proper execution plan.

I recall how we had decided upon 'Oil' as the topic for a cross-curricular project in Grade 11 in one of the schools

I taught. Subjects which contributed to the project were physics, chemistry, geography, history, mathematics, English and computer science. Every subject analysed and presented 'Oil' from its perspective, staying within the boundaries of the curriculum meant for Grade 11.

The Teacher as a Creative and Critical Thinker

Being a creative and critical thinker must become the way of life for all twenty-first century teachers. Only then will we be able to create a lasting impact on our students. Thinking out of the box is synonymous with unique, unconventional or divergent thinking. This comes not only from having a good command over one's subject but also by widening the horizon of the students by being able to connect the learning process with the community, the environment and above all the world. It is a challenge that can be tackled successfully with an open mind, being conversant with the latest resources and technology and above all, communication and collaboration.

Types of Learners: The VARK Model

Imagine a classroom. A geography teacher is teaching landforms created by fluvial (river) activities. The teacher begins by explaining what causes erosion and deposition along the river bed. She notices that a few students have

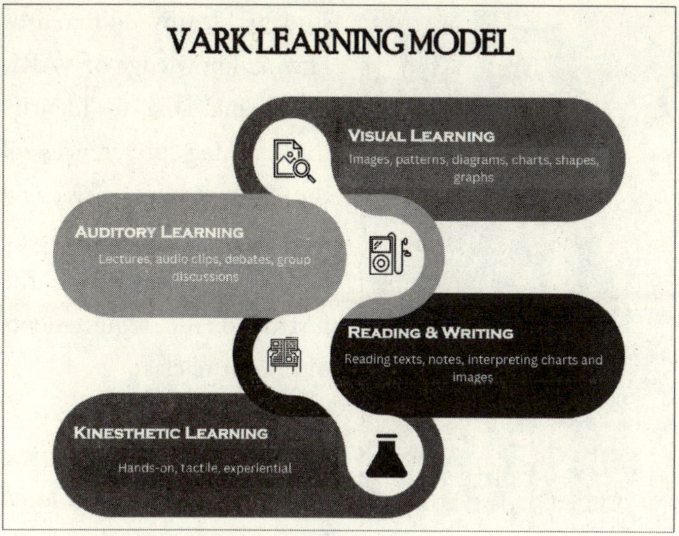

understood her explanations; they are auditory learners. She then draws diagrams of the landforms, shares real images and further explains the topic. The teacher observes that some more learners have started understanding the concepts; they are visual learners. She then asks a few students to read the related portion from the textbook, who are the 'read/write' kind of learners. Finally, the teacher uses Google Earth to trace the course of the River Ganga and the landforms created by it. The class looks at the live feed with awe, and the kinaesthetic learners understand the concept entirely.

This model of learning styles was shared by Neil Fleming in 1987. Standing for **Visual**, **Auditory**, **Read/Write** and **Kinaesthetic**, VARK describes different learning preferences of the students. As teachers, we need to understand that every

student learns differently. Having knowledge of VARK and being able to identify the learning preferences of the students in a class will help the teachers prepare lesson plans to cater to the instructional requirements of the entire class.

We need to think outside the box and look for teaching methods that can cater to all types of learners. Films are a great medium of communication for VARK learners. Short films or excerpts from films relevant to the topic being taught create a great impact on all the students. While teaching about hacking, I often showed a clip from Blackhat, *a 2015 film about a convicted hacker who helps authorities to track down a dangerous cyber-criminal.*

QR Code for the Clip from Blackhat

Similarly, the 2010 film The Social Network, *which narrates the launch of Facebook, can be a good warm-up exercise to introduce the topic of social networking in class. However, one needs to be careful and choose a visual aid only after careful screening. The clips need to be age-appropriate and relevant.*

In this context, I would like to mention the theory of Multiple Intelligences (MI) by Howard Gardner, which states that every human learns best depending on one's independent intelligence. The intelligences have been categorised as linguistic, logical-mathematical, spatial, musical, bodily kinaesthetic, interpersonal, intrapersonal and naturalist. In Book 1, I have explained how MI can be implemented in a classroom situation with practical examples.

I also want to share with you the mission of the International Baccalaureate (IB) programme: 'The IB develops inquiring, knowledgeable and caring young people who help to create a better and more peaceful world through education that builds intercultural understanding and respect.' This thought resonates completely with the objectives of NEP. Having said that, let us take a quick look at the IB Learner Profile, which translates the IB Mission statement into action. The profile aims to develop learners who are inquirers, knowledgeable, thinkers, communicators, principled, open-minded, caring, risk-takers, balanced and reflective. The purpose of sharing the above information is to give a fair idea of how to prepare ourselves to build citizens of the world.

For Further Reading on IB Learner Profile,
Scan the QR Codes

Chapter 4

Pedagogy and Learning Theories

> Teachers' beliefs are understandings, premises or propositions felt to be true about the educational purpose and the educational process.

The term pedagogy is coined from two Greek words: paidos, meaning child, and agogos, meaning leader. It refers to the methods teachers adopt to teach students in a class. Pedagogy depends a lot on the teachers' beliefs, understanding of the learner profiles, application of learning theories, student psychology, as well as a teacher's teaching style. Pedagogy is implemented successfully through meaningful interaction between the teacher and the learners in the classroom.

Learning theories are frameworks that try to understand and analyse the way humans receive, process and retain information. The guidelines thus offered provide clarity and direction to build one's teaching approach. All of us consciously or unconsciously apply one learning theory or the other in classroom transactions. However, a conscious approach empowers teachers to adapt to multiple learning styles and create an inclusive classroom environment favourable for learning. To become an effective teacher in the classroom, one must know how a child learns, their background and learning challenges, and then apply the appropriate learning theories to promote lifelong learning for each student in the class. Learning theories help the teachers communicate clearly with all the stakeholders, like the students, parents and the school administrators.

Continuous development in the field of psychology paved the way to learning theories like cognitivism during the 1950s, the Experiential Learning Theory (ELT) by David Kolb in 1984 and the most recent, connectivism, as the prevalent twenty-first century learning theory. In this book, we will discuss five basic learning theories in use. Each one of them emphasizes different concepts. However, as smart teachers, we must learn to blur the boundaries of these theories, combine concepts and come out with the best learning strategy that suits our classrooms.

This book is going to cover the learning theories, pedagogies and teaching tools that can make teaching computer studies fun and meaningful. Many learning theories have emerged over the years to provide frameworks for educators. However, there are some learning theories which every educator must be familiar with. Each theory differs in the priority of the concept it proposes.

Behaviourism

Behaviourism was propounded by John B. Watson, a renowned American psychologist, in his paper, 'Psychology as the Behaviourist Views It'. This learning theory states that a person's behaviour is formed through conditioning, which occurs due to the influence of his/her environment. The key features of behaviourism are learning through association/ external stimuli (classical conditioning), rewards and punishments (operant conditioning) and aversion therapy/ extinction of a behaviour.

Using reinforcements to get positive responses from the students is a good example of the application of behaviourism.

I always make it a point to keep aside five to seven minutes of class time and use gamification quizzes created by Kahoot! and Quizizz as an end-of-class activity. I feel this serves as feedback to the teachers on the degree of the students' understanding. Many teachers prefer using 'skill and drill' exercises in the classroom to get correct responses through regular drilling. Formative assessments, like short MCQ tests at the end of the lesson, are another way to measure student response. Based on the student response, a teacher can decide to repeat the topic in the next lesson with a different teaching approach. In the following chapters, you will find that every lesson has some activity as the end-of-class assessment.

Behaviourism may be applied through rewards and recognition to acknowledge students' responses as well as non-verbal cues (body language) for class management. In my experience, younger students are motivated when a smiley/star is put against their names on the 'How did I do in my computer studies class?' chart displayed on the class noticeboard. Older students, on the other hand, get motivated mostly with verbal cues like 'Good job, Sachin', 'Great Neena', 'Spot on, Sam' and so on. It is important to call out the student's name for them to feel special.

Cognitivism

Founded during the mid-20th century by Jean Piaget, a Swiss psychologist, cognitivism is a shift from behaviourism and focuses on internal mental processes, like how a human mind receives, processes, stores, organizes and retrieves information. The theory believes in the existence of a basic unit of knowledge, schema and the schemata, that are built gradually through active learning and problem-solving activities. In simple words, according to the cognitivists, the human mind is like a computer that continuously collects data externally, processes the data using problem-solving and thinking skills and generates new information for storage in the memory.

Active learning is a method where the students are encouraged to participate actively in the learning process by engaging in activities like brainstorming, discussion, problem solving, as well as creation. The learning experience is given more importance.

I have found that making the students conduct surveys to collect data and then analyse them to reach a conclusion is a meaningful learning experience. Let me share with you how I used a survey as a teaching tool for the students in Grade 6. I was teaching an international curriculum at that point, and I had to teach ergonomics to Grade 6. I was wondering how I can make such a dry topic like ergonomics interesting to the students. I began the lesson by asking the students whether they had noticed any difference in the design of seats between the old and the new cars. Students were excited to share their observations. I then went on to ask why they think modern cars have bucket seats. There came a volley of responses. I discussed the correct way to carry a school bag and why we should carry a bag in this manner. I asked the students why we need to have proper seating posture while using a computer and reminded them about 'touch-typing', which they were taught when they were in lower grades. At the end of all these examples, I introduced ergonomics to them, told them what it is and why it is important.

The students of the class were divided into groups of four, and each group was assigned a different topic to conduct a survey. The topics were ergonomics in all classrooms of Grade 6, in teachers' rooms, in the cafeteria, ergonomics of school bags and ergonomics of the shoes worn by the students to school. The entire process was divided into the following steps:

i. *Framing survey questions, which were finalised after my approval.*
ii. *Interviewing concerned people, at least 10–15 subjects had to be interviewed.*
iii. *Group-wise data collation in a spreadsheet, which was again supervised by me.*
iv. *Class presentation on findings.*

This activity was a great success. The students prepared charts on the correct seating postures while using computers, as well as while sitting in class. They made a presentation suggesting changes that should be made in teachers' room lighting and the rearrangement of seats in the cafeteria to make seating more comfortable. Based on their findings, some changes were made in different areas of the school.

I would like to describe the above activity to be a combination of cognitivism, Constructivist Learning Theory and Experiential Learning. These three learning theories stem from each other and are very close in their characteristics.

Constructivism

According to the Constructivist Learning Theory (CLT), knowledge is an intersubjective interpretation. Students construct new knowledge based on their previous knowledge (schema), experiences gathered from the environment, personal interpretations (reflection) and perceptions.

> **Cognitivism vs Constructivism**
>
> The major difference between Cognitivism and Constructivism is that Cognitivism talks about building on prior knowledge, while Constructivism talks about building new ideas and concepts based on personal experiences and interactions.

Jean Piaget believed in cognitive (radical) constructivism, whcreas Lev Vygotsky was a strong believer of social constructivism. John Dewey's ideas of constructivism had commonalities with both Piaget's and Vygotsky's theories.

According to Piaget, a child takes centre stage in the process of knowledge acquisition and creation. Piaget's research on children suggests that learning occurs through the process of assimilation, where the new knowledge is added to the existing schema. The schema is modified and updated with the new information by the process of accommodation.

Vygotsky, on the other hand, had emphasizcd the role of social interaction in knowledge acquisition. He believed that a child is born with the ability to develop cognitively. As the child grows and interacts socially with peers and others in his environment, there comes a considerable improvement in his cognitive process of cognition.

Vygotsky came up with the idea of the Zone of Proximal Development (ZPD), which suggests that learning

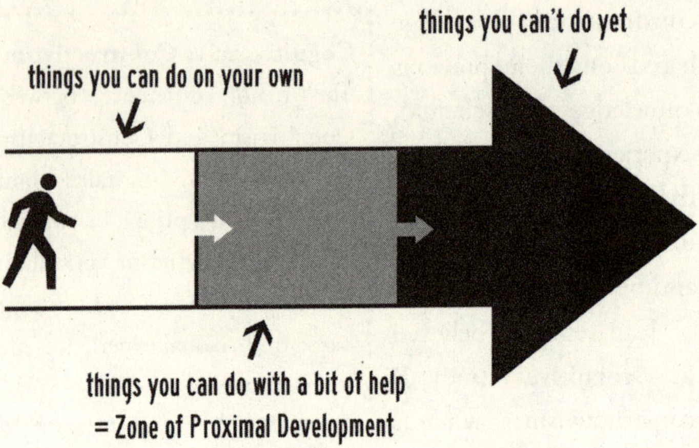

can improve drastically with the support of a 'More Knowledgeable Other' (teacher or peer). He categorized learners into three different types: can do on their own, can do with support and cannot do even with support. The key requirements of ZPD are 1) a knowledgeable and skilled guide, 2) scaffolding technique to make the learner self-reliant and 3) social interactions to help the learners build upon their skills.

Examples of CLT are:

- **Problem-Based Learning (PBL):** The objectives of PBL are to instil twenty-first century skills among the students by letting them answer open-ended questions by applying content skills. The students develop independence and an inquiring mind.

For example, the students of Grade 6 can be asked to create a blog or a podcast as an influencer to promote any one of the Sustainable Development Goals put forward by the United Nations that they are passionate about. This will give the students ample opportunity to research, brainstorm, find out the problems, the causes and how the problems can be mitigated. As is evident, PBL offers ample opportunity for the students to hone the 4Cs of learning as well as problem-solving skills.

As a part of an exchange programme with the students of a school in Germany, I guided the students of Grade 6 to create a collaborative Wiki on 'Festivals in October'. Our students described the Indian festivals, whereas the German students described the carnivals of Oktoberfest, the celebration part, of course, not the beer drinking part. A lot of communication went on between the students of both schools through the blog.

- **Inquiry-Based Learning (IBL):** IBL encourages students to ask questions, investigate real-world problems and come out with plausible solutions.

I recall one such project in which I was indirectly involved. To involve the students of Grades 9 and 11 in sustainable development, the environmental science teachers decided to convert an unused compost pit of the school into a vermi-compost pit. The students were given the responsibility to conduct the research work, to prepare the pit with the help of an expert, talk to the vendors to purchase earthworms, as well as conduct an awareness drive in school to request other students, parents and teachers to bring non-citrus vegetable peels regularly to feed the pit. The vermi-compost pit is running successfully, and the compost produced is being used in the kitchen garden of the school.

I still remember how the students worked sincerely on this project, and the knowledge they gathered was mostly hands-on.

- **Reciprocal Teaching/Learning:** It is an important strategy to improve comprehension skills in students.

Teaching ethics and cyber laws can be quite boring. I prefer using the reciprocal questioning method to introduce some fun elements during teaching by switching roles with the students. Based on their existing knowledge, the students work in groups to prepare questions to ask me, and I answer. Then it is my turn to ask questions to them, and they answer. The quizzing continues till we are all exhausted of questions. This method is quite helpful to identify the fuzzy points, things the students did not understand well and allows me to revisit the topics. There can be situations where the students ask questions for which we do not have answers. The best way to tackle these situations is to surrender and ask them to provide the answer, or else answer them the next day.

- **Cooperative Learning:** This is the strategy to form small groups of students and involve them in structured activities. Reciprocal teaching is a type of cooperative learning.

I have often used Think–Pair–Share activities in my classes. You will find the use of Think–Pair–Share in a few lessons described later. Learning to write correct algorithms is the first step towards developing problem-solving skills among students.

While introducing an algorithm to Grade 8, I always shared with the students steps to get ready for school or steps to prepare a sandwich, activities they are already conversant with. However, these steps were given to the students in a jumbled order. I would ask them to form pairs, think and arrange the given steps in the correct order. Pairs would come up with different answers, most of them correct. I would then explain that a problem may have different solutions; however, a programmer has to choose the most efficient one.

Scaffolding

It is an instructional process which the teachers may apply in the classroom to gradually remove support and guidance once they find the students have become confident and competent learners. Scaffolding comes in handy in cases where a difficult topic is to be introduced, to help students find information through research, monitoring student progress through formative assessments, group work, guided practice and many more circumstances.

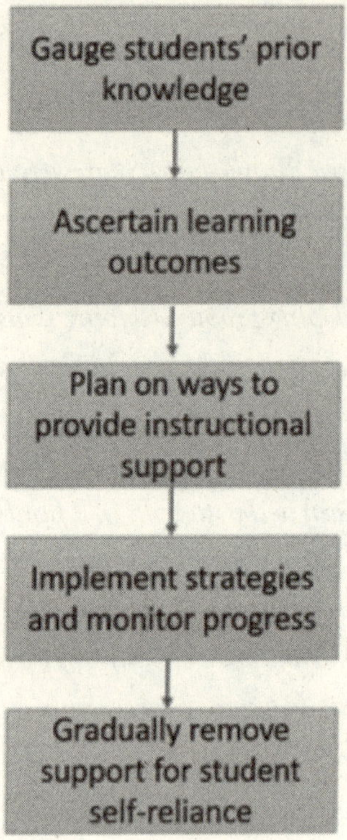

The scaffolding model is based on '**I do**' (Instructor does), '**We do**' (teacher and student work, peer work) and '**You do**' (the students work).

Let us imagine a lesson where we are introducing algorithm writing to the students. Since the algorithm is an absolutely new concept, after explaining what an algorithm is all about, we will write a small algorithm for adding two numbers. We explain the steps and rules at length to the students. To make their understanding clearer, we write another small algorithm

Connectivism

The advent of the digital revolution has affected all spheres of life, including education. Students gather knowledge not only from their teachers but also from online content available on social media, websites, blogs and podcasts. Developed around the year 2005 by Stephen Downes and George Siemens, connectivism is considered to be the learning theory of the twenty-first century, which caters to the needs of modern-day teachers and students. Although both Siemens and Downes are proponents of the theory, they differ in their focus areas. While Siemens has explored the role of social aspects in connectivism, Downes's focus has been on technological networks like non-human entities and machine-based learning.

Connectivism draws inspiration from earlier learning theories like constructivism and proposes that knowledge is distributed across a network of connections, similar to the concept of a computer network, with two main components – nodes and links. A node is supposed to be a repository of knowledge, which can be an expert in a particular domain, an organization disseminating information, a library, as well as an online forum or blog dedicated to a specific topic. A link, on the other hand, is a channel of communication or a bridge between two nodes through which knowledge is shared.

Siemens and Downes have put forward eight principles of connectivism as follows:

- Learning and knowledge rest in the diversity of opinions.
- Learning is a process of connecting.
- Learning may reside in non-human appliances.
- Learning is more critical than knowing.
- Nurturing and maintaining connections are needed for continual learning.
- The ability to see connections between fields, ideas and concepts is a core skill.
- Accurate, up-to-date knowledge is the aim of all connectivist learning.
- Decision-making is a learning process. What we know today might change tomorrow. While there's a right answer now, it might be wrong tomorrow due to the constantly changing information climate.

Connectivism in the classroom can be implemented through the use of social media, gamification, blogs, podcasts and simulations.

I prefer to use gamification apps like Quizziz or Kahoot! to prepare short quizzes to test the progress of the students during a class. Quite a long time back, I used Wikispaces, a free wiki hosting platform, for my students in Grade 6, to share class news on their Wiki. After Wikispaces was phased out, I used Doku Wiki and Media Wiki for my students. I have also taught interested students to create personal blogs to share their opinions on topics of their interest. These exercises create an atmosphere of excitement among the students. Apart from language development, it also helps the students become confident in working online with proper ethics.

In the subsequent chapters, an effort has been made to showcase the application of some learning theories/ pedagogies relevant to teaching computer studies in the middle school. The topics have been selected from the CBSE Computer Science and ICSE Computer Studies syllabus of Grades 6 to 8. Practical application of active learning strategies, such as classroom debates, discussions, gamification, role-play, flipped classrooms, simulations and many more, have been discussed. Wherever necessary, grading rubrics have been added.

Platforms like Google Classroom, Microsoft Teams, Edmodo or learning management systems (LMS) help facilitate interaction with the students or share lesson guidelines, helping in the implementation of blended learning in class. Most lessons have been designed keeping these platforms in mind.

The lessons have been planned applying Rosenshine's Principles of Instruction. Barak Rosenshine has put forward a set of evidence-based guidelines for improved learning outcomes and teaching practices. Many apply some or all of these principles in classrooms without being aware of their actual implications. The conscious application of these principles in the classroom will help achieve any teacher's desired learning objectives.

The principles are

1. Begin the lesson with a review of previous learning (recall).
2. Present new material in small steps (easy to process).
3. Ask a large number of questions (to all students to practice retrieval).
4. Provide models and worked examples (linking with known concepts leads to deeper learning).
5. Practice using the new material – repetition till the teacher feels the students are ready.
6. Check for understanding frequently and correct errors through direct questioning.
7. Obtain a high success rate – students move on to a new topic without any misconceptions of the previous one.
8. Provide scaffolds for difficult tasks (scaffolding has been discussed earlier).

Importance of Energizing the Mind and Body

I always made it a practice to make the students stand in their own places and dance to slow rhythmic music if my lesson was towards the end of the day. It would hardly take three to four minutes.

I often instructed them to wave their hands or lightly jog or rotate their ankles while being in their own places.

This would not only energize their minds but also reduce stiffness of their bodies from constant sitting.

9. Independent practice after support has been removed.
10. Monthly and weekly reviews.

It is always important to create a dynamic learning environment in your class. It gives you a sense of achievement if the students look forward to your lessons.

Be creative, and combine the essence of more than one learning theory suitable to teach a topic. Apply pedagogies as well as tools to make learning holistic that energises the mind, body and spirit of the students.

I know it is easier said than done. However, the present scenario demands that teachers mould the students to be twenty-first century ready. That cannot be done by simply cramming information into their brain. Help them hone skills necessary for today's world through your lessons. This can be achieved by:

i. Understanding the needs of the current generation of students.
ii. Honing the twenty-first century skills yourselves.
iii. Meticulous planning to implement appropriate learning theories and pedagogies in class.

Chapter 5

Constructivist Learning Theory (CLT)

Cross-Curricular Teaching and Role-Play in Action

CLT has been discussed at length in Chapter 4. However, let us recapitulate the concept. According to CLT, students construct new knowledge based on their previous knowledge, experiences gathered from their environment, personal reflection and perceptions. It is one of the most suited learning theories for the present-day education system as it stresses active learning, critical thinking and problem-solving instead of rote learning.

We can implement CLT in our classrooms through pedagogies like role-play, problem-based learning, cooperative learning, flipped classroom, interdisciplinary learning and many more. Let us look at an example lesson plan which implements interdisciplinary learning and role play.

Topic: Fundamentals of Computers

This lesson has been designed to cover components of a computer system: the processor, memory and storage devices.

Tools used: Jumbled word game, role-play, quiz.

Skills: Creativity, critical thinking, communication and collaboration.

Teaching pedagogy/strategy: Cross-curricular teaching, role-playing.

Interdisciplinary, also known as cross-curricular teaching pedagogy, stems from the Constructivist Learning Theory (CLT). This powerful approach creates greater learning during the stipulated class time by motivating students and strengthening their understanding.

I prefer using a warm-up or recall exercise as an introduction to most of my lessons, following Rosenshine's Principles of Instruction (refer to Chapter 4). For this lesson, I want the students to rearrange jumbled words to create meaningful sentences to understand the difference between data and instruction.

The jumbled word game will require you to collaborate with the English teacher of the respective class and collect several sets of sentences about different topics of grammar.

The following link may be used as a guide.

Jumbled Words Game Reference

I had the opportunity to share the staffroom with a couple of English language teachers. They helped me a lot, not only to frame the games but also with answer keys. Warm-up exercises such as these are always used to set the mood for the class. The students would look forward to the surprise activities I would throw at them in the middle of a lesson.

It is always challenging to make the students perform role-play. Initially, some would not take the exercise seriously. Some were shy, some were not very sure of the concepts learnt, and some simply didn't care. However, things changed when the students noticed how role-play was improving their retention capability. From then on, the whole class started taking part and playing their roles according to their abilities.

Warm-Up Exercise

Before delving into the components of a computer system, I would prefer to explain the difference between data and information. This can be done by making them play with jumbled words. Divide the students into groups of three. Hand each group a set of jumbled words to construct four to five sentences on a specific topic, and write them in their exercise books. Each group must call out the sentences they constructed after the stipulated time given to them. The teacher may then point out how the jumbled words are facts (data), but the words do not carry any meaning until they are rearranged to construct meaningful sentences (information).

Content Delivery

I think all the teachers will agree that the components of a computer system can be taught best with the help of the following diagram. I prefer to use the flowchart symbols to depict the input–process–output as this will help while we teach flowcharts.

Once the components of a processor are clear, it would make sense to refer to the game they played and ask the groups to write on chits of paper and submit them to the teacher, who played the roles of ALU, CU and memory in their respective groups while playing the game. The teacher may then choose random chips and ask the groups to explain their roles as ALU/CU/Memory.

While explaining cache and primary and secondary memory, we may discover that most students are already

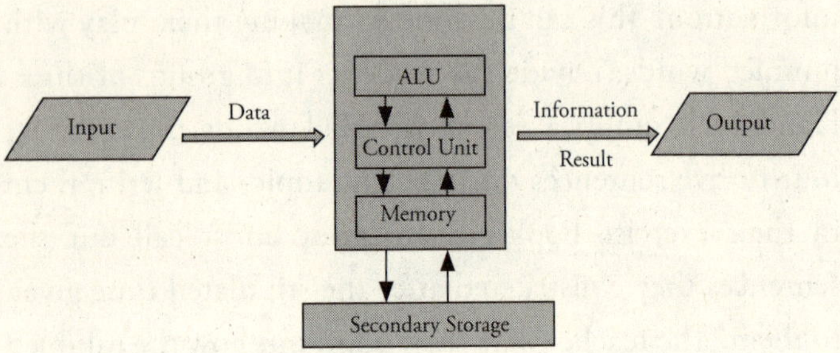

Components of a Computer System

aware of the concepts. The teacher may find it easier and more engaging by making this part of the learning an interactive question–and–answer session through the use of a quiz. We may use online quizzing sites like Kahoot!, Quizizz and Involve.me to easily create these resources and then make the students play in the class or generate printed sheets for the quiz.

Summing Up with the Creation of a QR Code

This exercise is to make the students understand the concept of permanent storage in an interesting and hands-on way. The teacher may demonstrate how to create a QR code for a website/YouTube video for the students. The students must note down the steps. There are several free online QR code generators like www.canva.com, www.adobe.com and more to choose from.

Home Assignment

1. Most students must be quite familiar with the Input/Output devices. Students must read the portion from their textbooks and be prepared to ask 'Who am I' questions in class the next day.
2. The students create a QR code linked to a website suggested by the teacher and mail the .png/.jpg file to the teacher. This may be graded.

Chapter 6

Flipped Classroom

Flipped Classroom, Peer Assessment and Paired Learning in Action

Topic: Input/Output Devices

The students are aware of I/O devices from earlier classes. There is no point in repeating these topics. I think applying the flipped classroom would make the class more engaging. Keeping this in mind, I had created a home assignment in Chapter 5 to create 'Who am I' questions, based on what they read from their books on I/O devices.

The students would need to apply analytical skills based on their prior knowledge and recent reading/research. I feel that, apart from assessment by the teacher, peer assessment would make the lesson more meaningful.

Tools used: Gamification – reward system and feedback.

Skills: 4Cs, social skills.

Teaching pedagogy: Flipped classroom, peer assessment, paired learning.

> **Flipped Classroom**
>
> 1. Students gain knowledge **before class.**
> 2. Students apply concepts learnt and get feedback **in class.**
> 3. Students gauge their understanding and extend their knowledge **after class**.

Quite self-explanatory, the flipped classroom is when the traditional classroom setting is flipped. The students come prepared to the class and take part in active learning through collaborative projects, discussions, debates, problem solving, reflection and so on.

The success of a flipped classroom depends on a lot of factors:

a) **Availability of Content:** The students must be able to access and go through the content before coming to the class. The contents may be prepared by the teacher or taken from textbooks, magazines, blogs and websites.

b) **Quality of Content:** This will decide the quality of in-class activities and the creation of meaningful 'Who am I' questions in this case.

c) **Planning of In-Class Activity and Support:** The activity to be conducted, like a debate, discussion or any other collaborative work, needs to be planned meticulously well ahead of the class. The teacher needs to facilitate the students as guides during the activity.

d) **Flexibility of the Teacher:** A lot depends on how flexible the teacher is during this exercise. An activity may not go as planned, and the teacher may have to improvise something immediately for the success of the lesson.

During a planned flipped classroom session on the real-life applications of 'iterations', most students in my class were unable to explain with proper examples. I helped some of them by giving them hints, and yet others with real-life examples of iteration and asked them to come up with something similar. I understood that flipped classrooms must be implemented with topics with which the students are comfortable.

Peer assessment is another learning tool that enhances the students' evaluation skills and helps them provide feedback. If implemented properly, it makes the students think critically, be more involved in classroom learning as well and be a responsible learner.

The grading rubric must be explained and shared with them at the beginning of the lesson. Grading sheets have to be distributed to the students. By drawing lots, each student has to pick an I/O device topic to frame the 'Who am I' question. Preparation time of five to seven minutes may be allotted. Students must be allowed to use their textbooks or other resources. When a student presents a question, the teacher needs to select a student from the student audience to identify the device in question.

Paired learning, when combined with the flipped classroom pedagogy, is a powerful tool for deeper learning and engagement. The paired students will be able to discuss their understanding of the topic, clarify each other's doubts (peer tutoring) and then create 'Who am I' questions with clues. Paired learning strategy may also be implemented during paired debates, role play as well as Think–Pair–Share activities.

Note: You need to ensure that both members are contributing meaningfully during the activity. Apply differentiation and give adequate support to the individuals or pairs who are struggling. The support may be in the form of providing additional reading materials or videos, or allowing the students to work according to their comfort without simplifying the requirements of the activity.

> **Differentiation** is a teaching technique that allows teachers to cater to individual student needs, based on their learning style and degree of understanding. The goal is to keep all the students engaged.

Flipped Classroom Implementation

Ask the students to pair up quickly. Have chits ready from before with the name of one I/O device on each. Distribute the chits to each pair to frame one 'Who am I' question with clues. You may have to repeat topics depending on the number of pairs.

Please ensure that you can finish the entire exercise in one lesson; otherwise, the excitement will die down, and students will lose interest. Adjust the preparation and presentation time to be allotted to the students accordingly.

Find below samples of grading rubrics for both teachers and students, and a grading sheet for the students.

GRADING RUBRIC FOR THE STUDENTS

Excellent (A)	1. The clues were fun and challenging. 2. We could easily identify the device.
Good (B)	1. Clues shared were borrowed directly from the textbook. 2. We could easily identify the device.
Average (C)	1. Some clues were missing. 2. We could somehow identify the device.

Rewarding students with digital badges is an effective motivational tool.

To know more about badging best practices and ways to create badges you may visit:

https://www.techlearning.com/how-to/motivating-students-with-digital-badges

https://www.classcraft.com/blog/how-to-create-a-digital-badging-program-in-your-classroom/

GRADING RUBRIC FOR THE TEACHER

The teacher may choose to design digital badges.

Suggested Badges	Suggested Grading Pointers
Rockstar!	1. Demonstrates excellent understanding of the topic. 2. Applied critical thinking and creativity.
Super!	1. Demonstrates good understanding of the topic. 2. Tried to apply some critical thinking and creativity.
Good Job!	1. Understands the topic. 2. The question framed had insufficient information.
Well Tried!	1. Has little or no understanding of the topic. 2. Had difficulty framing the 'Who am I' question.

WHO AM I GRADE SHEET FOR THE STUDENTS

Graded by: ______________________ Class and Section: ____

Student Name	Device chosen	Excellent Grade A	Good Grade B	Average Grade C

Summing Up

At the end of the lesson, you need to sum up by giving general feedback on the students' performance, providing positive reinforcements as well as areas which need improvement. You also need to bridge the gaps left by the students. It would be a good idea to invite an English teacher to evaluate the overall presentation, language, concept and creativity.

Instructions for the Next Class

The students have been learning about the History of Computers since they were younger. Reiterating the topic in the class is pointless. You may plan to implement this topic by applying collaborative as well as hands-on learning (experiential learning) in the next lesson. Both pedagogies fall under Constructivist Learning Theory.

> **Experiential Learning** pedagogy links real-world experiences to theoretical knowledge. Hands-on learning ensures development of 4Cs as well as increased engagement and retention.

Divide the students into six groups and assign each group the following topics and the activities they will have to come prepared with for the next class. Please try to group the students according to their abilities or learning styles, or readiness for the topics. Allow flexible grouping so that students can work in their comfort zone.

1) **Early Calculating Devices:** Abacus, Napier's bones, Pascaline, analytical engine, etc. The students may present role-play as the inventors, or they may create models and demonstrate the functioning of the abacus (basic arithmetical operations) and Napier's Bones (simple multiplication). If the students have an abacus, they may bring it to the class for demonstration.
2) **First-Generation Computers:** ENIAC, vacuum tubes, Alan Turing, machine language, etc. The students may present about the features, advantages and shortcomings of these devices through a presentation or chart.
3) **Second-Generation Computers:** Emergence of transistors, magnetic core memory, difference from first generation, assembly language, etc. The students may present a short skit on how things improved in the second generation.
4) **Third-Generation Computers:** Development of integrated circuits (IC). A group discussion on 'How ICs have revolutionized the world of electronics'.
5) **Fourth-Generation Computers:** Invention of microprocessors, semiconductor memory, etc. The students must create a timeline of the developments made during this period.
6) **Fifth-Generation till Recent Times:** Cloud computing, AI, robotics, etc. Using AI to compose a song on the advantages and disadvantages of the developments in

the fifth generation, use a fitting tune for the song and sing in the class.

Assign three to five minutes of presentation time to each group. Students from other groups may ask questions at the end of each presentation. The students must be graded not only on the quality of their presentation but also on how they answered audience questions. You may even grade the quality of questions asked by the student audience. Since the activities will be quite interesting, you may invite teachers as observers or judges. You may want to record the activities for future reference. Grade the students using a grading rubric and offer positive feedback as well as point out areas that could be improved. A sample grading rubric for you is shared below.

Grading Rubric for Presentation on the History of Computers

Total Points = 30	**Meets the Criteria 100 per cent (5)**	**Meets the Criteria Partially (3)**	**Does Not Meet any Criteria (1)**
Presentation is visually appealing and complete			
Presentation is organized			

Member participation
Group cohesion
All the members clearly understand the topic
Satisfactory Q and A session

Chapter 7

Experiential Learning Theory (ELT)

Visual and Collaborative Learning and the Experiential Learning Cycle in Action

Influenced by pragmatism, cognitivism and constructivism, psychologist David Kolb proposed the Experiential Learning Theory (ELT), trying to tie together experiences, cognition, emotions as well as environmental factors as major influencers in the process of learning. ELT has quite a few similarities with constructivism. Both theories believe in constructing knowledge through experience, reflection and experimentation (contextual learning). You'll find more details in Chapter 4.

In this lesson, we will implement Kolb's Experiential Learning Cycle while teaching embedded computers. It is a four-stage cycle that promotes learning

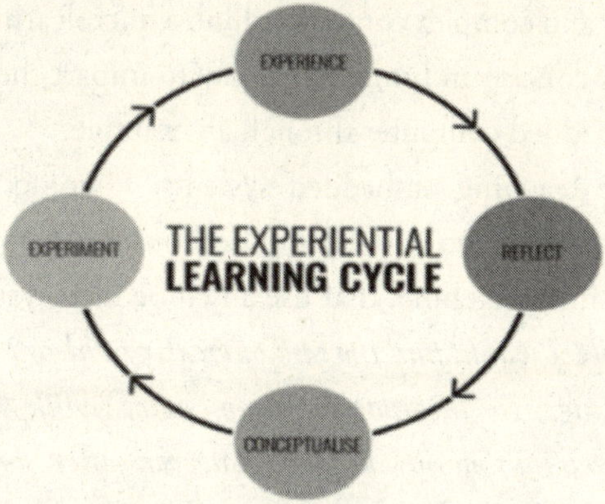

through experimentation, experience, reflection and conceptualization. We will also use visual learning in this lesson, a powerful tool for better engagement, understanding and retention by the students. It can be implemented using graphs/charts, infographics, mind maps, videos, pictures as well as flash cards. We are going to use a microlearning video to introduce the topic.

Prerequisites for this Lesson

It is best to conduct this lesson in the AI/robotics lab.

1. Microlearning Video

We will introduce the topic with a microlearning video. Let us try to understand what microlearning is first, which has gained popularity because of its focus on a small piece of content out of a larger and complex content. I think a microlearning video is an easy, concise and interesting way to impart the concept of an embedded computer through an example.

Before teaching embedded systems, I would want to create a small video on any of the household appliances, like a washing machine, that use an embedded system.

Initially, I would find the task of creating videos to be quite intimidating. To incorporate commentary while recording a video was out of my league. However, after some failed attempts, I got a hold of the concept and finally started creating small videos using KineMaster, PowerDirector, etc. However, to master the art, I took help from some students who used to represent the school in such competitions. They were only too glad to help. We must accept the fact that being a computer teacher does not always mean that we know everything that starts with 'C'. Taking help from the students creates a special bond with them. The advent of AI has changed the scenario. Free text-to-video websites create amazing videos suiting our needs. However, they curb our creativity.

The best way to create a video would be to create it using a mobile phone, which shows the basic functions and User Interface (UI) of your washing machine or any other embedded system in your home, with captions and commentary. You must give a brief basic explanation on the functioning of the system, mentioning the use of sensors within the video itself.

There are numerous video editing apps like KineMaster, iMovie, PowerDirector, Adobe Premiere Rush, etc., available for both Android and iOS, which you may use. If you are a beginner, you may take the help of apps like Loom (refer to https://www.loom.com/blog/microlearning for more information). You may also take the help of AI text-to-video generator websites like Invideo, instadoodle.com, playablo or VideoGen. However, they may not completely serve your purpose. The duration of the video must be within three to five minutes.

2. Planning for an Interdisciplinary Activity

At the beginning of the semester, you need to consult with the environmental science teacher to identify some simple embedded systems that the students may create to solve problems related to their local environment. Some project ideas could be a water wastage alert system, a smart plant watering system, a smart garbage collector and so on. Please involve the AI and robotics teacher and other teachers who can help the students in the implementation of these projects. A manual containing a problem statement may be created for each project that will act as a starter guide for the students. This document must also include a list of different sensors and their purpose. Some examples of actuators and their purpose may also be shared.

An interdisciplinary activity at this scale always requires meticulous planning. We need to remember that the projects must be in sync with the curriculum and integrated seamlessly into our lesson plans. We also need to appreciate that other teachers involved in the project must find the projects essential for their subjects as well. The first time I took part in such a project required all the involved teachers to sit for multiple brainstorming sessions before coming up with the right project topic, oil. For this project, I made the students analyse and interpret the data they collected for other subjects by using a spreadsheet application.

The students must be grouped carefully and have a mix of different kinds of learners in each group. The students must be aware of their group members before the class.

Each group must be handed a coloured chart paper. They must bring their pastel colours, sketch pens, etc.

Topic: Embedded Computers

Tools used: Microlearning video, brainstorming, cross-curricular activity, ChatGPT.

Skills: Critical thinking, creativity, communication and collaboration.

Teaching pedagogy: Visual and collaborative learning, experiential learning cycle.

Introduction Using Microlearning Video

Begin by showing the microlearning video. You may pause the video at places to add some more points. Make sure you share this video with the students on **Google Classroom** or **Microsoft Teams** after the lesson as a ready reckoner. Soft copies of the project manuals must also be uploaded.

You may ask questions to the students about the purpose of sensors in different fields like automated doors, elevators, cars, medical equipment and traffic signals. A simple block diagram of an embedded system may be shared and explained at this point to aid the students in the collaborative projects they are going to undertake.

It would make sense to mention some specific sensors and how they work, like in smoke detector, a burglar alarm, a sensor on an elevator door, an escalator and weather forecasting.

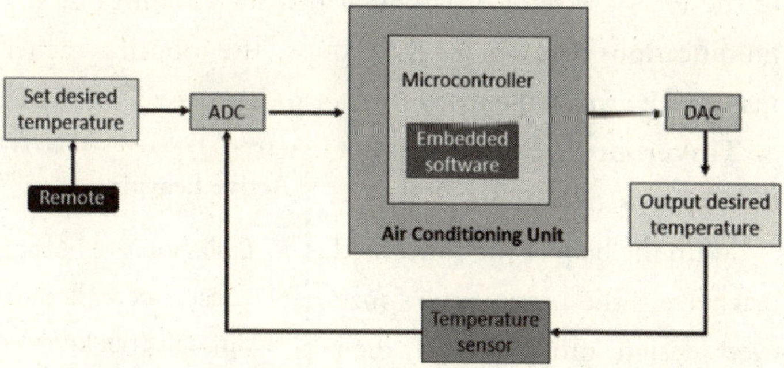

Simplified Block Diagram of an Embedded Air Conditioning System

In-Class Activity

Brainstorming

Please distribute the project manual with the problem statement to each group. The students must read them, brainstorm within their groups and then try to conceptualize an embedded system that may solve the given problem. They must draw a block diagram of the system with the necessary sensors and actuators. The teachers who were responsible for framing the problem statements must be present. The role of the teacher will be that of a moderator and facilitator. You all need to move from group to group to observe the progress, and may facilitate a group if you feel necessary.

Allow 15 minutes for this exercise. The groups must submit their ideas at the end of the exercise. You have to be very encouraging while discussing the ideas shared by each group with the class, and must mention that none of the ideas are right or wrong at this stage. Point out any modifications required for the groups. The robotics teacher may make arrangements to let the students use **Tinkercad** or **Tinkerbot** to design and code their proposed solution.

With the help of the concerned teachers, the students may even design prototypes of their conceived device for the end-of-year exhibition/class project.

Active Learning

- Collaborative learning.
- Create new knowledge through prior knowledge.
- Learn to analyse and evaluate.

Often, students try to speak over each other to dominate the group or establish his/her idea as sacrosanct. I laid down rules for brainstorming to control chaos during the session. I always told them before the session that everyone must take turns in sharing ideas, there is no such thing as a good idea or a bad idea – sharing one's idea is most important, they should not digress from the topic and always consult a teacher when in confusion. Although it was sometimes difficult to tone down their excited chatter but these rules worked well.

> Brainstorming is an effective tool to help students generate creative ideas based on theoretical knowledge and existing practice.

Important Points for the Success of the Experiential Learning Project:

1. Ensure collaboration with subject teachers.
2. Divide the development cycle into several stages. Stages for each group may vary.
3. Set a deadline for every stage and ensure that it is followed.
4. Review at the end of a stage with the other teachers involved and give feedback to the students
5. Be flexible, and allow students to modify at all times.

The objective is to help students become creative and experiential learners.

Chapter 8

It's ELT Again!

Experiential Learning with Role-Play, Mathematical Manipulatives and Poems

I have introduced the number system in this chapter. The topic has been divided into three lessons, and different tools of learning have been introduced to teach in each lesson.

Topic 1: Introduction to the Number System

Let us try to experiment with storytelling, mathematical games and role-play to teach the number system.

Storytelling is an effective way to convey facts and information to all kinds of learners in a classroom. A visual learner tries to create mental images while listening to a story. An auditory learner gathers knowledge from the facts shared in the story. A kinaesthetic learner gathers feelings from the emotions shared in a story. Information shared in a story can be easily retained for a long period. A story can be an arrow in your quiver for student engagement and joyful learning.

I love storytelling sessions. It works well with all age groups. A well-planned story can be used to successfully teach a topic. In order to ensure complete engagement from the students, I often asked students to note down keywords or points during the session. I would ask the students about the words or phrases they noted and whether they could share some information on them.

Mathematical games can be a useful tool that can be implemented at the beginning, middle or end of a lesson to introduce a topic, as Brain Breaks or to summarize a theme. Apart from being engaging, these games enhance the problem-solving and critical thinking skills of the students.

Role-play is another powerful tool that promotes social skills like communication and empathy. It enhances classroom engagement, creativity, imagination and confidence of the learners.

Tools used: Mathematical games, storytelling.

Skills: Counting, matching, sequencing, critical thinking and logical reasoning.

Teaching pedagogy/strategy: Experiential learning, role-play.

Requirements for Place Value Role-Plays

Please get the props for two role-plays, which must be planned well in advance of the class.

1. Select four students to represent the four place values of the decimal number system.
2. Give them two chart papers cut into half to represent four place value cards of the decimal system – 1s, 10s, 100s and 1000s.
3. Instruct them to write '**10^0 – 1s (units), 10^1 – 10s (tens), 10^2 – 100s (hundreds) and 10^3 – 1000s (thousands)**' on each card.
4. Now, select six students to represent six place values of the binary number system.
5. Give them three chart paper cut in half to represent six place value cards of the binary system.
6. Instruct the students to draw 1, 2, 4, 8, 16 and 32 big dots on those pieces of chart paper so that the dots are visible till the end of the classroom.
7. At the bottom of the dots on each card, they must write '**2^0 – 1, 2^1 – 2, 2^2 – 4, 2^3 – 8, 2^4 – 16, 2^5 – 32**'.

Sample Binary Cards

I chose this easy game from the following resource and made some modifications. There are printable cards as well as several worksheets to choose from on this website.

https://classic.csunplugged.org/documents/activities/binary-numbers/unplugged-01-binary_numbers.pdfIntroduction through Storytelling:

Students love stories. Well, I took inspiration from ChatGPT 4.0 to generate the framework of the story on the number system. I have filled in the gaps and edited the story wherever necessary to create a compact one, as you see below.

Purpose of Number Systems

1. Computers understand only binary digits.
2. It is difficult for the humans to remember long series of bits while working on computers.
3. Old 12-bit computers mostly used Octal, which groups three bits, 2^3 for computer applications. They are used in aviation industry and limited computing.
4. For 32- and 64-bit computers, use hexadecimal numbers as it groups four bits, 2^4. They are compact and can accommodate more numbers on a computer.

The Journey of Numbers: A Story of the Number System

Long, long ago, when there were no paper and pencils, people didn't have any idea about numbers like we do today. However, they **still needed to count** – sheep, fruits and even days.

So, they used stones, sticks and marks on cave walls.

The Tally Marks

In a small village, a shepherd named Arin tied knots in ropes to count his sheep. One knot was equal to one sheep. When the knots got too many, he started making **tally marks** on stones.

But soon, he started wondering, 'Can there be a better way?'

The Romans Created Counting Symbols

Far away in ancient Rome, people created symbols like I, V, X and L to count. It was clever but tricky.

For example, **IV = 4**, **IX = 9**, and **X = 10**.

'But where's zero?' Arin wondered.

The Roman system had no zero – and counting big numbers was difficult.

India Added the Mathematical Marvel, Zero

Meanwhile, in ancient India, the brilliant mathematician Brahmagupta came up with the concept of zero. Aryabhatta and Brahmagupta together developed a new number system – using digits from zero to nine. They gave the world something no one else had thought of: **zero**.

Suddenly, math became powerful.

Now everything made sense with 10, 100 and 1,000!

This system travelled through Arab traders to Europe, and the world adopted the Hindu–Arabic number system, the decimal number system we use today.

The Binary Revolution

Many centuries later, computers were invented. But these machines couldn't understand 0 to 9 – they only understood ON and OFF, or one and zero.

And so, the binary system was created.

1 = ON

0 = OFF

This became the language of computers, phones, games and more.

Octal and Hexadecimal Followed

Representing numbers using the binary system was quite complicated as it involved the use of a lot of zeroes and ones. Then came octal and hexadecimal to make binary numbers compact and easy to understand.

What We Do Now

We use these number systems for different purposes.

From knots to codes, numbers have come a long way – and they keep growing with us.

Moral of the Story

Numbers are more than symbols. They are tools created by humans to understand, measure and shape the world around them.

You may now highlight the prefix – bi, deci, octa and hexa, plus decimal (suffix) – to explain the base and the range of digits for each number system. It is also necessary to explain briefly the purpose of each number system. Please find below a mind map for the same.

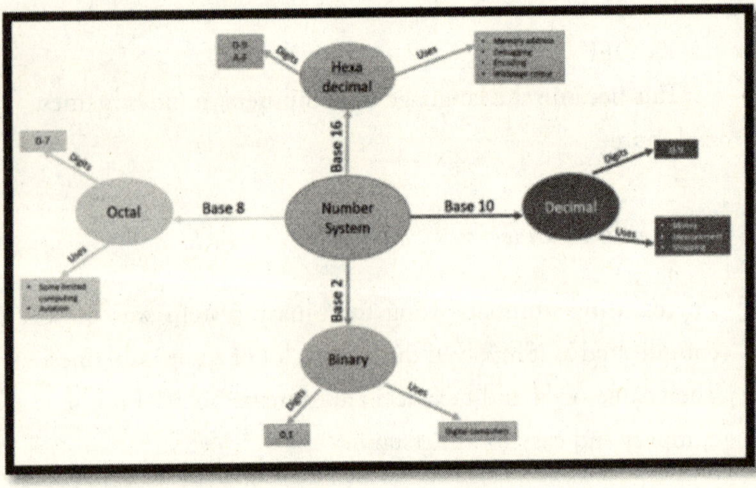

Mind Map on Number Systems; Created with PowerPoint

Post this, you may play 'Fun with Numbers' with the students. Write down random numbers on the board, like 101, 235, 23AF and ask the students to identify the number system they represent. As is evident, the first two numbers belong to multiple number systems. At this stage, you may talk about how to distinguish numbers by adding their bases as subscripts.

Time to play 'True or False'. Write down some more numbers on the board, this time with their bases and ask the students whether they are correct or not. For example, $(234)_2$, $(1010)_8$, $(595)_8$ and $(595)_{10}$. Encourage the students to support their answers with reasons.

Understanding the Progression of Numbers

Before introducing the students to the binary equivalent of decimal, octal and hexadecimal numbers, it would be better if they understand how the numbers progress. They must understand that in any number system, adding one to the highest single-digit number will lead to the lowest two-digit number and so on.

For example, adding 1 to 9_{10}, the highest single-digit number of the decimal system, will yield 10_{10}, the lowest double-digit number.

Similarly, adding 1 to the highest two-digit number, 99_{10}, will yield 100_{10}, the lowest three-digit number.

Students must understand that the same rule applies to other number systems as well.

For example, adding one to 1_2, the highest single-digit binary number cannot be two. It will be the lowest two-digit number, 10_2.

Therefore, $7_8 + 1 = 10_8$, $F_{16} + 1 = 10_{16}$

Time to introduce the students to the binary equivalent of other number systems. The students need to understand that the number of bits required to represent one digit of another number system will be N, where $2^N <=$ base of the other number system. For example, octal has a base of eight, which is equal to 2^3. Therefore, an octal digit will be represented by three bits. Similarly, decimal (base $10 < 2^4$) and hexadecimal (base $16 = 2^4$) will both be represented by four bits.

Role-Play 1 – Decimal Place Value

Please instruct the four students who prepared the place value cards for the decimal number system to stand in a row in front of the class with the cards facing the class.

Call out a decimal number, like 408, and ask any one student from the audience to say which cardholders must step forward. In this case, the hundreds and the units cardholders are going to step forward. Instruct the student to construct the number 408 on the board using these two cards and show it to the others in the class like this: 4x100 + 10x0 + 8x1 = 408.

I know, it seems like a silly game, but it would be far easier and faster if you could simply show it to the class yourselves. However, making the students get involved in the learning process would ensure better engagement and learning.

Role-Play 2 – Connecting the Dots

Please ask the five students who have the dotted cards numbered 1 to 16 to stand in front of the class with the dotted sides visible to the class. The student holding the card with 32 dots must show the blank side to the class. The sequence of the cardholders, as is evident, will be from one dot on the left to 32 dots on the right.

Interaction and Exercises to Sum Up the Class

The teacher asks:

- Is there a sequence in which the number of dots is increasing? (Increasing in multiples of two.)
- What would be the number of dots on the sixth card? (As soon as the students answer, the sixth student flips the card.)

The teacher states, decimal numbers can be obtained by adding the number of dots on the cards.

- Which cards will be required to derive 12? (Cards with eight and four dots.)

Instruct the students with the unused cards to flip the cards to make the blank sides visible to the class. Inform the class to write in their exercise books zero for each blank card and one for each card with dots visible in a left-to-right sequence of the cards.

The result is 12_{10} = 001100, which is the binary equivalent of 12.

Ask the students: what would be the highest and the lowest number using these six cards? (63 and 1).

Give them some more numbers to work out, which will use one or more cards.

In-Class Assessment

Complete the blank spaces in the following chart.

Hint: keep adding one to generate the next number.

Binary Equivalent of Decimal, Octal and Hexadecimal

Digits	Decimal	Octal	Hexadecimal
0	0000	000	0000
1	0001		0001
2		010	
3			
4	0100	100	0100
5			
6	0110	110	0110
7			

8		
9	1001	1001
A (10)		
B (11)		
C (12)		
D (13)		
E (14)		
F (15)		

Home Assignment

1. Why do we need three bits to represent octal numbers?
2. If the binary code of 'A' is 1000001 and that of 'a' is 1100001, then what will be the binary code of 'Hi'?
3. Nina wants to use "Adding the dots" game to find the binary equivalent of 82.
   i. How may dotted cards would she need?
   ii. What will be the number of dots on the leftmost card?
   iii. Which dotted cards will be added and what will be the binary value?

Topic 2: Place Values, Conversion to Decimal Number System

Mathematical manipulatives are hands-on tools used to make abstract mathematical concepts easy to learn through visual as well as physical exploration. I am using an interactive place value chart as a manipulative in this lesson, as the concept of place values in other number systems can be tricky.

Tools used: Mathematical manipulatives – place value chart.

Skills: Counting, matching, sequencing, critical thinking and logical reasoning.

Teaching pedagogy/strategy: Experiential learning.

Requirements for the class: A week before the class, the students must be informed to get chart papers in four different colours to draw place value charts of four different number systems on differently coloured charts.

> Manipulatives are objects like blocks, dices, counters or charts, that are manipulated by students to learn mathematical concepts hands-on.

Explanation of Place Value Using Place Value Charts

For Whole Numbers

Please instruct the students to draw a table with four columns on a chart paper. The header must resemble the adjacent picture to

Place Value Chart Base 10			
1000	100	10	1

represent units: 10s, 100s and 1000s. Ask them to use pencils. Provide the students with some whole numbers in the decimal system and ask them to place the digits in appropriate columns.

Time to explain that the place values of the digits in a whole number are factors of its base, beginning from the right with $base^0$ and increasing towards the left as $base^{N-1}$, where N is the number of digits. Please use some concrete examples to explain, and ask the students to rewrite the header of the earlier chart with place values as seen in the adjacent image.

Modified Place Value Chart			
103	102	101	100

Following this principle, the students must now be able to draw place value charts for four-digit binary, octal and hexadecimal numbers on other coloured chart papers. Provide them with some numbers of different number systems to fill in the place value chart.

For Numbers with Decimal Places

With the help of examples, explain how the place value system works for numbers with decimal places.

	Place Value Chart for fractions					
$(345.78)_{10}$	10^3	10^2	10^1	10^0	$1/10=10^{-1}$	$1/100=10^{-2}$
		3	4	5	7	8

The students must now modify their place value charts to accommodate numbers with decimal places.

It will be easy to teach conversion to decimal from other number systems using these place value charts.

Number Conversion

I find this image quite useful to explain number conversion.

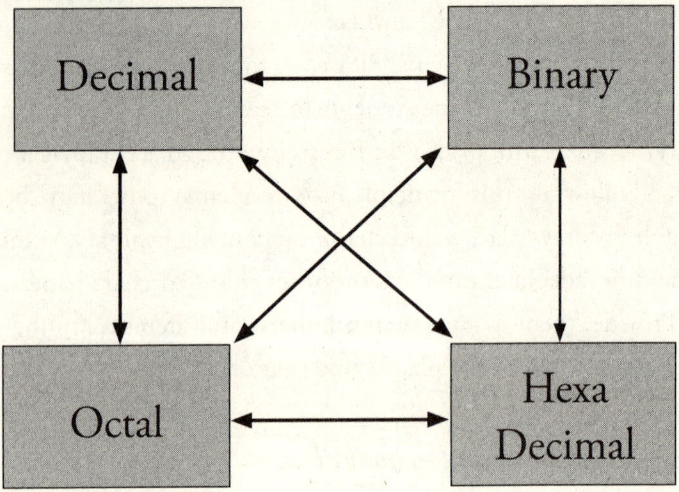

Conversion Between Different Number Systems

Conversion to Decimal from Other Number Systems Using a Place Value Chart

No.	Binary Place Value Chart				Decimal Equivalent
	2^3	2^2	2^1	2^0	
101_2		$1X2^2$	$0X2^1$	$1X2^0$	$4+0+1=5_{10}$
	Octal Place Value Chart				
101_8		$1X8^2$	$0X8^1$	$1X8^0$	$64+0+8=72_{10}$
	Hexadecimal Place Value Chart				
$10A_{16}$		$1X16^2$	$0X16^1$	$10X16^0$	$256+0+10=266_{10}$

Rules for Conversion:

1. Multiply each digit in the place value chart by its corresponding place value.
2. Add the values to get the decimal equivalent.

End of the Lesson Formative Assessment

A sample questionnaire for your reference:

1. State whether the following are valid numbers in their respective number systems. Give reasons:

   a) $(873)_8$ b) $(1001)_{10}$ c) $(1119)_{16}$ d) $(A25)_2$ e) $(928)_{10}$
2. What will be the next number?

   a) $(11)_2$ b) $(17)_8$ c) $(5C)_{16}$
3. Using a place value chart, convert the following numbers to base 10.

   a) $(11001)_2$ b) $(674)_8$ c) $(FE3)_{16}$ d) $(62.51)_8$

Topic 3: Other Conversions

I often use self-created poems or make the students help me create one to make learning fun and engaging. Moreover, the rhyme, rhythm and mnemonics in a poem help the students to reinforce concepts, the number system conversion in this case, easily. In this lesson, I have taken the help of an online poem generator website to create a poem on grouping digits before conversion.

Tools used: Mathematical manipulatives – a division chart and an online AI poem generator.

Skills: Counting, matching, sequencing, critical thinking and logical reasoning; social skills – conversation, communication and listening.

Teaching pedagogy/strategy: Experiential learning, Think–Pair–Share.

Recall Exercise

1. Using the symbols × and √ create as many combinations as possible, and fill in the following table. One combination has been given for you.

× × √

2. How many combinations could you create?
3. Did you apply any rules to create the combinations?

Binary to Octal or Hexadecimal

The students have already learnt about the binary equivalent of octal and hexadecimal numbers in the first topic of this chapter. So, teaching them grouping and replacing each group of bits with the respective octal or hexadecimal digit will be easy. Sometimes students find it easier to remember rhyming poems. I created one for the rules of grouping using bardaifree.com There are many other online AI poem generators.

Rules to Convert from Binary to Octal/Hexadecimal

1. Start grouping three or four bits from right to left.
2. If there are additional bits to the left, add leading zeroes to complete a group.
3. Replace each group with its equivalent octal/hexadecimal digit.

Poem created using bardaifree.com

From right to left, we start our quest,
Grouping three or four bits, we do our best.
If more bits remain, fear not, my friend,
Leading zeros we add, to make amends.

Examples of conversion:

$1101_2 = (15)_8$

Step 1. 1 <u>101</u>

Step 2. <u>001</u> <u>101</u>

Step 3. <u>001</u> <u>101</u>
1 5

$101101_2 = (2D)_{16}$
Step 1. 10 <u>1101</u>
Step 2. <u>0010</u> <u>1101</u>
Step 3. <u>0010</u> <u>1101</u>
2 13 (D)

Decimal to Binary, Octal and Hexadecimal Conversion

The students would have become used to charts by now. Using a chart for this operation will keep their work neat and minimize the chances of mistakes.

Decimal to Binary

Division operation	**Quotient**	**Remainder**
35/2	17	1 LSB
17/2	8	1
8/2	4	0
4/2	2	0
2/2	1	0
1/2	0	1 MSB

$\therefore 35_{10} = 100011_2$

Why do we divide a decimal number with the base of the other number system?

Division by the base will always yield digits valid for that number system.

Example: for base eight, division by eight will always result in remainders from zero to seven, which are the digits valid for octal system. Same goes true for the other number systems.

Decimal to Octal

Division operation	Quotient	Remainder
35/8	4	3 LSD
4/8	0	4 MSD

$\therefore 35_{10} = 43_{8}$

Why is the last remainder the MSD/MSB?

Applying the Euclidean division method, we keep dividing the quotient (q) by the base (b) of the other number system and record the remainders (r) till q>0.

$q_i = q_{i+1}.b + r_i$

Applying the above rule in the following example, we get:

$35_{10} = [r_5r_4r_3r_2r_1r_0]_2 = r_5x2^5+r_4x2^4+r_3x2^3+r_2x2^2+r_1x2^1+r_0 = 1x2^5+0x2^4+0x2^3+0x2^2+1x2^1+1x2^0$

The last remainder, r_5 is the MSD as it has the highest place value.

Decimal to Hexadecimal		
Division operation	**Quotient**	**Remainder**
159/16	9	15 (F) LSD
9/16	0	9 MSD

$\therefore 159_{10} = 9F_{16}$

End of the Lesson Exercise

Octal to Hexadecimal and Vice Versa

For this exercise you may use the Think–Pair–Share technique. It is a powerful strategy for collaborative learning which yields deeper understanding.

Give the students the following problems:

1. $(457)_8=(?)_{16}$
2. $(DF26)_{16}=(?)_8$

Step 1. Give the students two to three minutes to think about how to solve the problems.

Step 2. At the end of three minutes, ask the students to pair up with their neighbours, discuss their methods and decide upon the

> **Think–Pair–Share**
>
> 1. Think individually.
> 2. Brainstorm in pairs.
> 3. Share learning with class.

easier method. Give them another three to five minutes to complete the exercise.

Step 3. Now, select a random pair to come to the board and explain the method they found best. Find out how many others agree. If there are pairs who disagree, call them to the board to explain their procedures.

Home Assignment

Along with other home assignments, you may want your students to play any one of the following games and share a screenshot of the level they cleared.

- https://learningcontent.cisco.com/games/binary/index.html
- https://games.penjee.com/binary-bonanza/

Chapter 9

Cognitivism, Constructivism and Multiple Intelligence (MI) Theory Combo

Visual Learning Through Mind Map and Timeline

Visual learning tool is a perfect fit in cognitivism (helps in effective mapping of information in the brain), in constructivism (helps in constructing new knowledge), as well as aids visual learners according to Howard Gardner's MI Theory.

Topic – Classification of Computers According to Size and Purpose

Tools used: Visual learning tools, including mind maps and timelines.

Skills: Critical thinking, creativity, communication and collaboration.

Teaching pedagogy/strategy: Visual and collaborative learning, video pedagogy.

In this lesson, we will use a mind map and a timeline as visual learning tools. **Mind Map** is a creative tool to organize large information in a structured and easy-to-understand manner. It usually begins with the main topic at the centre, then branches out to sub-topics at the next level, followed by further details at lower levels. What makes it concise and easy to remember is the use of keywords or small phrases, colour codes as well as icons or images.

Mind Maps

- Organize large information concisely.
- Easy to think, gather knowledge, collate ideas and remember.

I prefer using Canva or Mindmeister or even PowerPoint to create mind maps. However, it can easily be drawn impromptu on paper or directly on the board. Please encourage students to create and use mind maps to summarize chapters for better learning and understanding.

Guide for the Students to Create a Mind Map

1. Select the topic of the mind map and write it at the centre of a sheet (A4 size, landscape).

2. Identify three to five key features or points about the topic and write them around the topic in a circular manner with sufficient spaces in between.
3. Connect each feature/point with the topic using lines.
4. You may need to repeat Steps 2 and 3 for each of the key points
5. Use different colours for each sub-topic/point and the connecting lines for easy identification.

At first, let the students create a simple mind map. They can go on to create a mind map infographic once they feel confident. I found this wonderful infographic on how to create a mind map at https://www.thethinkingbusiness.com/mind-mapping/mind-mapping-intro.

It is quite eye-catching, don't you think?

Simple Mind Map

Mind Map Infographic

The students must also know how to read a mind map. Here is a little guide for your reference.

Reading a Mind Map

Step 1. Begin from the centre. That is the topic.

Step 2. Now, follow any of the connecting lines. It will take you to a sub-topic.

Step 3. The sub-topic may further branch out to features of the sub-topic.

Step 4. Repeat steps 2 and 3 until you finish reading all the sub-topics.

Mind maps can be quite useful for teachers as well as students for brainstorming, followed by decision making, before beginning any activity. It makes learning easier for the students as they can use this tool to take class notes as well as use a mind map as a reference during presentations.

Timeline, as we all know, is useful to record historical events or milestones in chronological order within a specific period. It makes it easy for the learners to view the period of a sequence of events and remember for later reference. Although the timeline is used frequently to teach history, it will come in handy to summarize the history of technological evolution as well. Timelines may be created either vertically or horizontally, depending on your creativity and space requirements. A couple of samples for you to refer to are below.

Learning to create a timeline is far simpler than that of a mind map. Depending on the number of events or

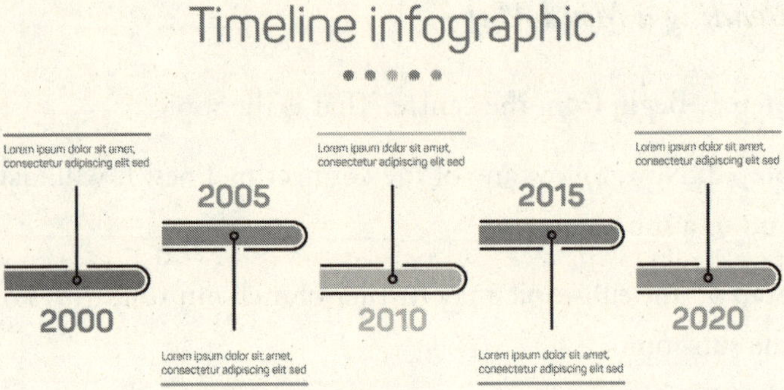

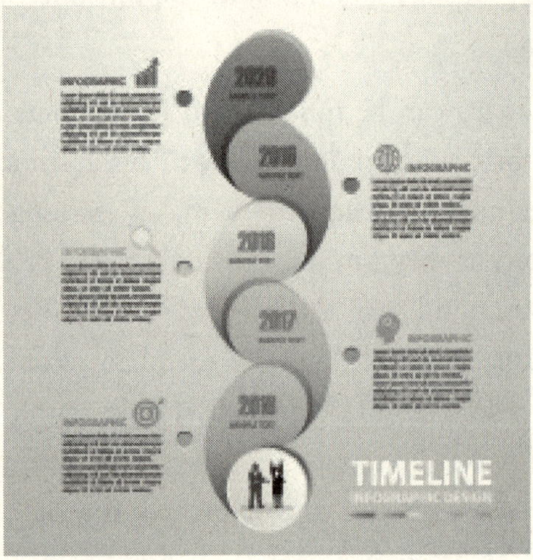

milestones, one needs to decide whether to use landscape or portrait orientation.

Steps to Draw a Basic Timeline

Step 1. Decide upon the number of events to depict on the timeline.

Step 2. Draw a straight line across the page.

Step 3. Draw small vertical lines at regular intervals for each event.

Step 4. For each event, mention the date/year and write a brief note

Apart from representing past events, students may use timelines to mark milestones of completion of a project.

Introductory Exercise

You may create a slide as below, or use a spreadsheet or Word document to carry out the following exercise.

Instructions for the students: Look at the following table, which contains seven digital devices. I will now be asking you questions about each device. You will answer each question according to my instructions.

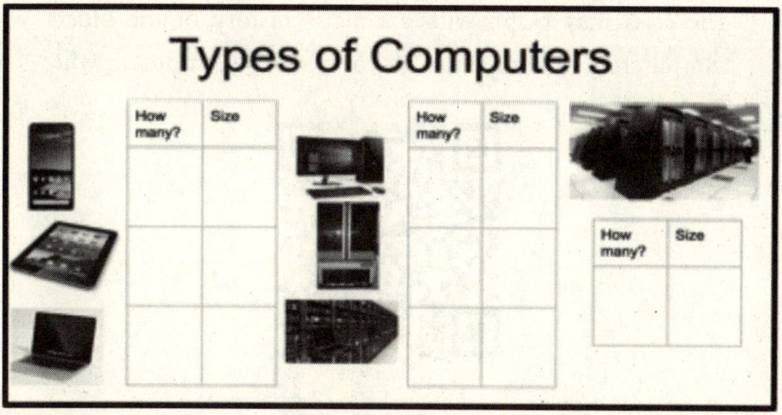

You may begin with the column '**How Many**' by asking the following questions, and fill up the respective column with the number of students who raise their hands.

How many of you have: 1) Smartphones, 2) Tablets, 3) Laptops, 4) Desktops, 5) Minicomputer, 6) Mainframe computer and 7) Supercomputer at home?

The number of students raising their hands for desktop computers will be less, and for mini/mainframe/supercomputer, it will be zero.

It is a good idea to ask the students at this point why the numbers dropped so much. You may add relevant reasoning at this time.

Next, the students may be asked to identify the largest to the smallest devices from the images, and you write numbers one to seven in the '**Size**' column based on the student's response.

Content Delivery

The class may begin with a concise history of the older computers. Showing brief videos of early computers will

PDP-1 Demo at the CHM (Short Version)

What Is a Supercomputer?

Chapter 1 Mainframe Computers and Minicomputers | Computer Class 6

make the interaction lively. Scan the QR codes below for some references in this regard.

You may now use a mind map to describe the features of ***any one*** type of computer you discussed during the introductory activity. A mind map on smartphones created with Canva has been shared for you.

Now, to involve the students in the process of creating the mind map, you may draw or display an incomplete

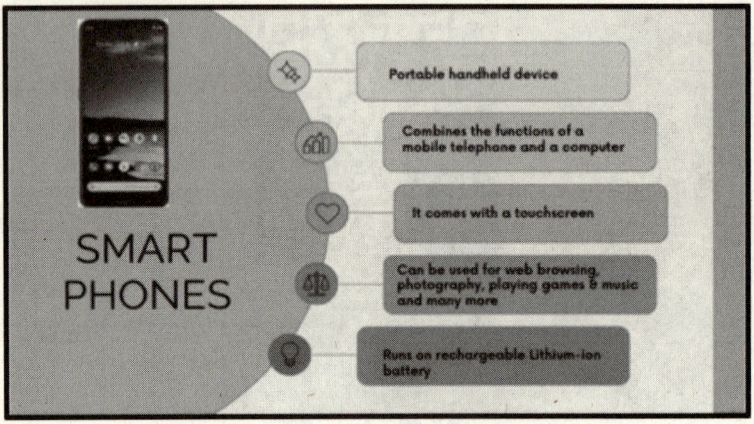

A Sample Mind Map on the Features of Smartphones

mind map and urge the students to help you complete it. As you can see, the following mind map is incomplete.

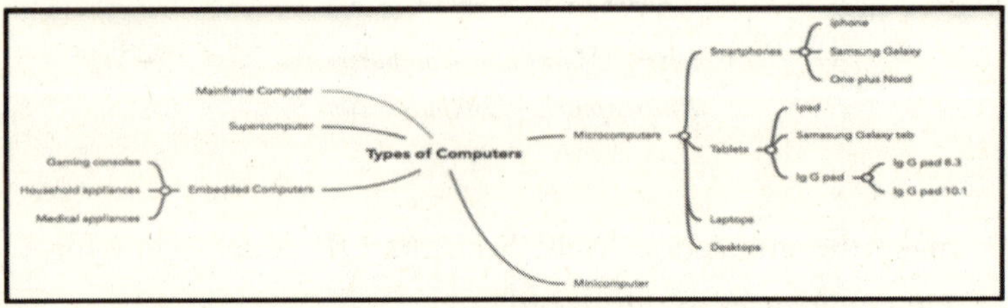

A Sample Mind Map on the Broad Categories of Computers Created Using www.mindmeister.com

In the absence of a smart board, you can create mind maps on the board too.

In-Class Activity: Mind Mapping

Pair the students, assign a type of computer to each pair to create a mind map (either on a computer or on an exercise book) on the assigned topic. They may use the textbook as a reference. The mind maps shared earlier must be on display for the pairs to refer to. The activity must be corrected and graded.

Home Assignment

Create a timeline on the types of computers that will include the name of the first computer of each category, the year of manufacturing and the name of the manufacturer(s).

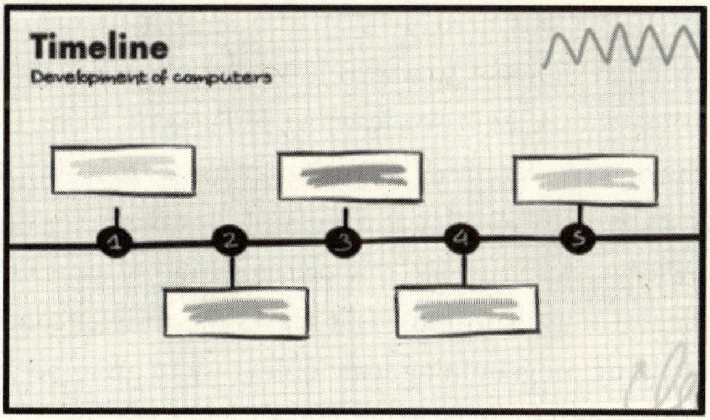

A Sample Structure of a Timeline Created with Canva; Can Be Shared with the Students

Please note, teaching a mind map may take your entire lesson.

Chapter 10

Constructivist Learning Theory and Vygotsky's ZPD

Case-Based, Paired Learning in Action

This chapter has been divided into smaller lessons, and we will use different strategies in the lessons based on the requirements. Case-based learning pedagogy is being used in the first two lessons. This pedagogy has its roots in CLT, focuses on active learning and uses real-life cases to construct knowledge. All of us use this pedagogy in our classrooms while teaching algorithms, as it makes the abstract concept of building programming logic quite easy to grasp because of the use of simple, relatable and real-life scenarios.

Coupled with the **paired learning** strategy, it enables students to grasp the concept of how to solve a problem in a step-by-step manner.

We are also going to use **HOTS** to help students apply their knowledge and develop creativity, problem-solving and critical thinking skills to gauge their understanding of the concepts taught. You will find in many of the lessons I have tried to cram in some HOTS as end-of-the-chapter or home assignments.

A **comic strip** is another visual learning tool that comes in handy to introduce abstract theoretical concepts. It makes complex concepts like algorithms easy to learn. As comic strips follow a definite structure and sequence, students grasp the logic of sequencing quickly.

I have divided the chapter into six lessons to segregate the topics and the related pedagogies. You may need more than one lesson to teach one topic.

Introduction to Algorithms and Sequencing

Tools used: Think–Pair–Share, HOTS, comic strip.

Skills: Logical reasoning, critical thinking, collaboration, creativity, communication.

Teaching pedagogy/strategy: Case-based learning, paired learning, visual learning.

Case-based learning is a student-centred learning where the students apply prior knowledge to real-life scenarios and create new knowledge.

Lesson 1: Algorithms

To add some zing to the lesson, I like to introduce algorithms with a comic strip. I have created the following comic strip of a boy, Pinocchio, whose mother has asked him to go to the kitchen and prepare a glass of fresh lime soda. Show the comic strip to the students and ask them to identify the steps Pinocchio took to prepare the drink. I have used https://app.story-boards.ai to generate the comic strip. I opened the website and was prompted to type in a storyboard, and the images were generated for me. What a blessing!

I am sure the students must be able to identify the steps: 1) Pouring soda, 2) Adding lemon juice, 3) Adding sugar syrup, 4) Ice, 5) Mint leaves and finally 6) A lemon wedge.

Please encourage them to write the steps in their exercise books.

Once the exercise is over, it will be easy for you to explain to the class that an algorithm is a step-by-step approach to solving a problem. Please ask the following questions to gauge the degree of understanding of the students.

1) What was the problem that Pinocchio faced?
2) How many steps did he need to solve the problem?
3) If the sequence of the steps is changed, do you think the problem would be solved? If yes, which steps can be shuffled?

Share some real-life examples to ascertain the importance of algorithms in daily life as well as in the field of computing and mathematics. Please discuss the rules for writing a simple algorithm with **start**, **stop** and **step numbers**.

Let the students pair up and understand the sequence in the algorithm through a worksheet on two real-life activities. The following is a suggested worksheet.

Assignment 1

The following pictures depict four steps for preparing cup noodles. The steps are not in order. Look carefully at each picture and in Column 2, state the action it describes in the process of noodle making. In Column 3, write the correct step number.

Steps to Make Cup Noodles	Describe the Action	Write the Step Number

Give the students five minutes to finish the first assignment. Ask a few students to call out their answers. There may be two different answers: some mark pouring hot water as Step 1 and seasoning as Step 2, or vice versa. At this point, you may explain that a problem may have more than one solution. Usually, the most feasible one is chosen for software development.

Assignment 2

Please ask the students to study the following scenario in their existing pairs and write down probable answers in the worksheet.

Jatin's father wants to change the password of his Google account. Jatin told his father to 1) Click on the profile icon on his Google account, 2) Select 'Manage your Google Account', 3) Go to 'Personal Info', 4) Choose 'Password' under 'Other Info' and 'Preferences for Google Services', 5) Verify it is you by typing in the existing password, 6) Type in the new password twice and click on change password button.

Jatin's father could not proceed beyond Step 5. What could be the probable reason(s)?

Probable answers could be:

1. Jatin's father has forgotten his existing password.
2. He is typing in an incorrect password.

3. He is not taking care of the case sensitivity of his existing password.

As is evident, there may be multiple correct answers. Summarize the answers with your input.

This exercise intends to let the students understand that even if Jatin's father followed the correct steps, he was still unsuccessful in completing the task because of the wrong input. This is something that, as programmers, we need to take care of through a process called **data validation**. Data validation flashes warning messages to let the user know there is a problem with the input. Students must appreciate that even the best algorithm fails without correct input.

Please utilize the rest of the lesson to let the students practise some simple, more real-life-based algorithms, like getting ready for school, sending an image as an attachment and some more activities, if time permits. This can also be a paired activity. Please call some pairs to share their algorithms, while the other students can share better alternatives.

Home Assignment

1. Write an algorithm to change your DP on WhatsApp.
2. Write an algorithm to take a screenshot while using Microsoft Word. Can there be an alternative to the algorithm you have written?

Lesson 2: Introduction to Flowchart: Sequencing

Once the students are conversant with the concept of simple algorithm writing, it will be easy to introduce a flowchart. I prefer making the students draw some fun flowcharts before showing them actual flowchart symbols.

Tools used: Think–Pair–Share, the calculator app, fun games, HOTS.

Skills: HOTS, logical reasoning, critical thinking, collaboration, creativity, communication and research.

Teaching pedagogy/strategy: Case-based learning/hands-on learning, peer review.

Recall exercise (the list is indicative):

The students pair up and write an algorithm for any one of the topics below:

1. To make a glass of hot chocolate.
2. To send an email to five friends.
3. To send a broadcast message on WhatsApp.

Assign five to seven minutes for the above task. You may now ask each pair to exchange the algorithm they wrote with their neighbouring pair. Each pair analyses the algorithm written by the other pair. Then, they form a group of four and brainstorm to decide upon the best solution (a five-to seven-minute exercise). The groups of four may modify their previous algorithms after brainstorming. They submit the final algorithm, which must have the names of the four participants. You may decide to ask a couple of groups to come up and explain the outcome of their brainstorming.

Introductory Exercise (Five Minutes)

You may begin teaching a flowchart with the following exercise.

The image below has all the steps necessary to make a cucumber sandwich. Each step is written in a rectangular box; however, they are not arranged in a sequence. There are two additional oval boxes – start and stop – to indicate

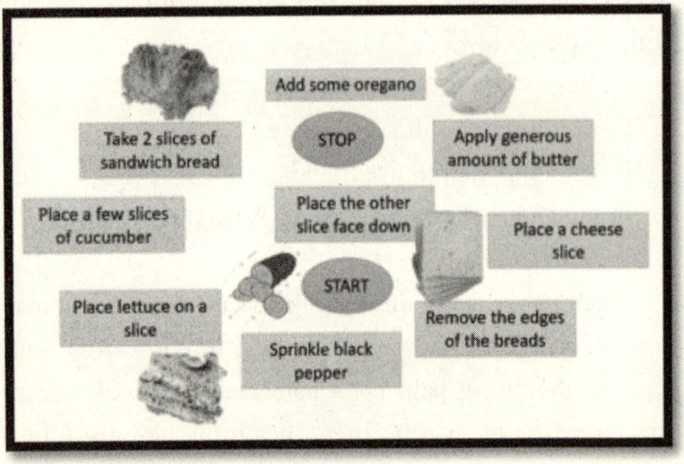

Steps to Prepare a Cucumber Sandwich

the beginning and end of the process. The image also has some additional frills in the form of ingredients; ignore them. Apply your knowledge to draw the boxes (both oval and rectangular) in correct order in your exercise book to prepare a cucumber sandwich. Join the boxes with arrows to depict the process flow.

Note: *it is important that the students understand the purpose of flow lines and use them as per norms. I used to have a tough time making students understand why flow lines cannot be directly connected to a flowchart symbol during iteration or decision-making.*

You may call upon a few pairs of students to draw their flowcharts on the board. Take opinions of the student audience and add your feedback, and ask the students to make necessary modifications.

Tell the students that they have successfully drawn a flowchart without even knowing what it is. Encourage them to define a flowchart, and whether drawing a flowchart is better than writing an algorithm.

As of now, it makes sense to explain the basic symbols used to draw the above flowchart – **Terminal and Process** symbols. The students will not be able

I prefer discussing the following only after the students have learnt all the flowchart symbols.

Symbol	Input Lines	Output Lines
Start	0	1
Stop	1	0
Process	1	1
Decision	1	2
Connector	1	1

to relate to the other symbols unless they know decision-making and iteration. The students must also understand the purpose of flow lines. Please help the students grasp that the following flowchart defines the stages of software development.

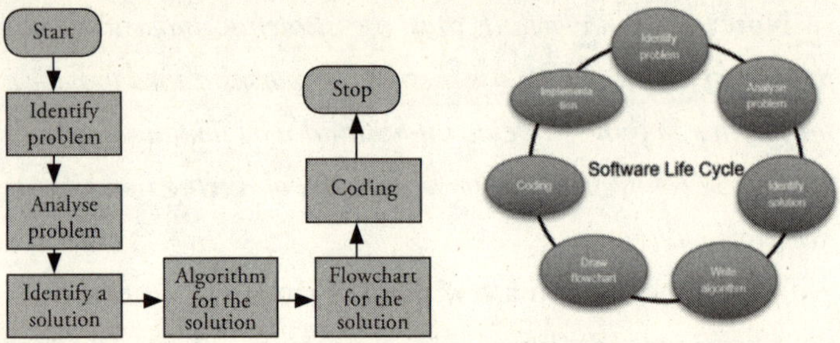

Flowchart for Stages in Software Development

Please ask the students to identify and name the symbols used in the above image (Flowchart for Stages in Software Development) to ensure that the students have understood the concept.

It is also important to make the students understand that there are constant upgrades

> **For Ready Reference**
> In April 2025, Google released Chrome 135 for Android, Windows, macOS and Linux.
>
> The latest stable release of Android OS, Android 15, came out in September 2024.

to existing software. That is why new versions are released by software companies periodically. This must explain the image, 'Stages in Software Life Cycle'. I have purposefully removed the testing and implementation stages from the cycle, as they will make things more complex.

At this stage, you may introduce algorithms for some arithmetical operations which require coding.

You may choose to discuss the steps performed for the addition operation by the calculator app. It might be interesting for the students if the addition operation of the calculator app can be shown on a smart board during the explanation.

Addition Operation on a Calculator

Algorithm **Flowchart**

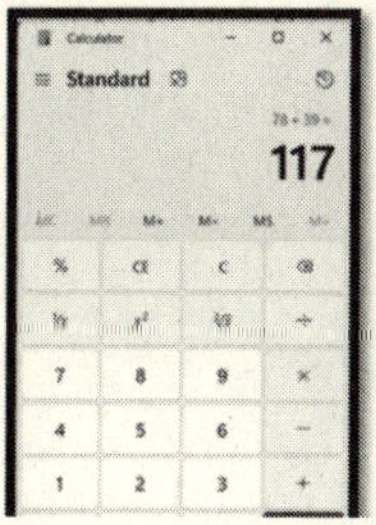

1. Start.
2. Open calculator app.
2. Type the first number.
3. Press '+' sign.
4. Type the second number.
5. Press '=' sign.
6. The answer is displayed.
7. Stop.

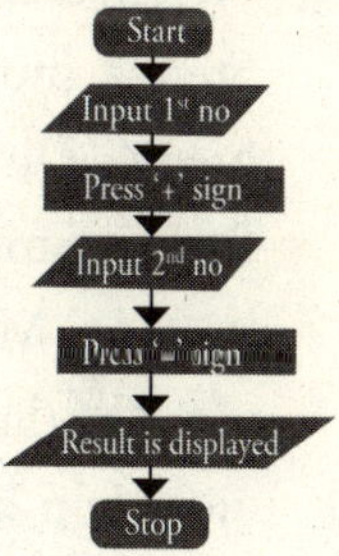

Regarding the above algorithm and flowchart, you may introduce the concept of storage of values in the memory of the calculator.

Summing-Up Assignments (HOTS):

It would be a good idea to sum up this lesson with questions to stimulate critical thinking and HOTS of the students.

1. Mina is trying to write a program to input two numbers and find out the results of addition, subtraction, multiplication and division. She has written the following algorithm.

   Step 1. Start.
   Step 2. Input the first number, A.
   Step 3. Display A + B.
   Step 4. Input the second number, B.
   Step 4. Display A x B.
   Step 5. Stop.

   i. Has Mina missed writing any step?
   ii. Are the steps in order?
   iii. Help her draw the flowchart for the complete and corrected algorithm.
2. The following flowchart is to calculate simple interest and print it. Convert it into an algorithm.

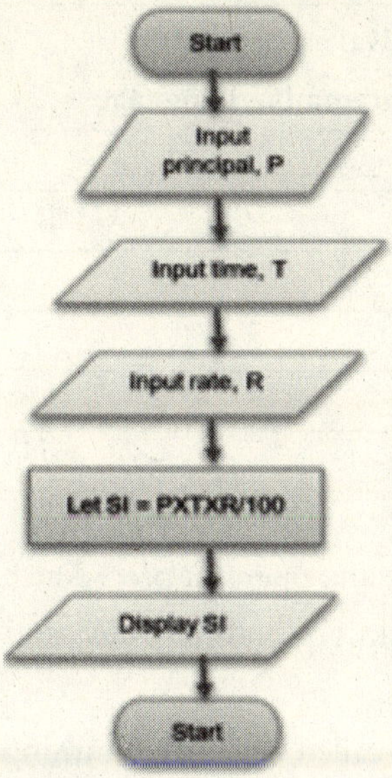

Why are we using labels like P, T and R to represent values?

It is easier to refer to the values by shorter names. During programming, these values need to be stored in computer's memory. The memory being huge in size, we name the location where they are stored to easily retrieve them – the address of our house makes it easy for people to locate us.

Home Assignment

In order to help the students hone crucial twenty-first century skills like critical thinking, problem-solving, information and digital literacy, I prefer that the students do research work as part of their home assignment.

1. Research arithmetic operators used in programming languages from the following link, and complete the table.
   https://www.iitk.ac.in/esc101/05Aug/tutorial/java/nutsandbolts/arithmetic.html

Arithmetical Operator	**Equivalent Symbol in Programming Language**
+	
-	
x	
÷	
To calculate 24	
To calculate remainder of 5÷2	

2. Research on the PEDMAS rule and operator precedence from https://www.geeksforgeeks.org/bodmas-rule/ and answer the following questions.
   i. What are the brackets called in programming languages?
   ii. How will you write the following expression in computer-readable form: **2 ÷ [{(5 +4) (8-3)} 6]**
   iii. In the formula SI = PxTxR/100, is there a need for brackets? Explain.
3. Prepare yourself from the links shared with you for teaching your friends the PEDMAS rule and precedence of operators.

Flipped Classroom in Action

We have already used the flipped classroom for earlier topics. As you may have instructed the students to research BODMAS and PEDMAS rules as a home assignment in the previous lesson, it is necessary to find the outcome of their research. Otherwise, the purpose of the exercise fails, as the students take the activity casually. You may organize a very short introductory session where you ask some students (peer teachers) to share their findings and engage other students to judge the quality of explanation offered by their peers. You need to wrap up the session with your feedback. I am taking the liberty of naming this session a byte-sized flipped classroom.

Lesson 3: Introduction to Decision-Making and Selection

Tools used: Think–Pair–Share, peer review.

Skills: HOTS, logical reasoning, critical thinking, collaboration, creativity, communication, research.

Teaching pedagogy/strategy: Flipped classroom, paired learning.

Introduction: Implementing Discussion-Based Byte-Sized Flipped Classroom

This session will take about 15 minutes of your class time. It involves explanation by the chosen students, the student audience acting as critics, and you offering feedback. Select a few students who you know will be able to explain the concepts clearly, ask them to come up to the front and explain to the class a question related to the contents of the previous lesson or BODMAS and PEDMAS rules based on the research they did at home. Some questions are suggested for you.

a. Did you find any difference between BODMAS and PEDMAS rules?
b. Do you think there is any difference between the following expressions: P*T*R/100, (P*T*R)/100, P*T*(R/100)
c. How would you write the following formula in a computer-readable form: $(a+b)^2 = a^2+b^2+2ab$?
d. Can you write algorithmic steps after 'stop' while writing an algorithm?
e. Why do you think it is necessary to write an algorithm and draw a flowchart before writing a code?

You must correct students if you find flaws in their understanding. However, proper caution must be taken not to hurt their ego or sentiment. *Continuous encouragement is the keyword.*

Decision-Making/Selection in Algorithm and Flowchart

Explaining the concept of decision-making gets easier when we do that with the help of daily life examples. Time to introduce a decision box.

The Concepts

Teaching the algorithm and associated flowcharts together will help the students understand the concepts better and will take less teaching time. You may even allow them to write the respective code. However, I prefer the traditional method of software development: algorithm – flowchart – coding.

You may decide to involve students in understanding that the actions of a decision cannot hang the way they are doing in the above examples.

A couple of decision statements and related flowchart snippets for you to share with your students:

*If it is cold outside, then put on a jacket otherwise carry a jacket.

*If your age is more than 17, you can vote. Otherwise, you can't.

Showing a flowchart and algorithm together makes it easy to grasp.

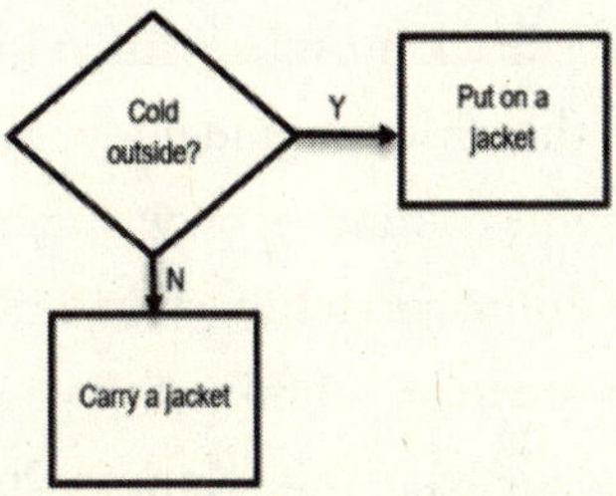

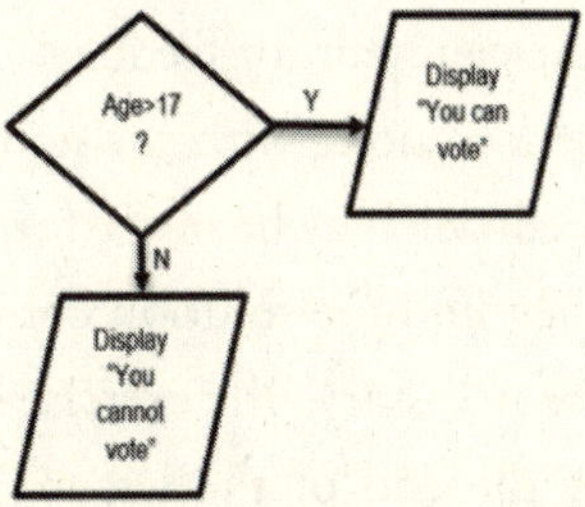

Assigning a few more exercises for better understanding of the decision-making concept using the strategy of Think–Pair–Share would be an excellent idea.

You may allow the students to think individually about the given problem, pair up, discuss and write algorithms and draw flowcharts. Some suggestions:

i. Imagine you are a food critic. You have been invited to a restaurant to review a new dish on their menu. You can pass any of the two comments depending on the taste of the food: 'Gastronomic pleasure!' or 'Someone please serve me real food!' Write an algorithm and draw a flowchart for the same.

ii. You have gone to watch a movie with your parents. After watching the film, give your verdict on the quality of the movie – Highly recommended :) or Absolutely boring :(– algorithm and flowchart, please. If time permits, assign a problem closer to coding as below.

iii. Write an algorithm and draw a flowchart to input two numbers and print the greater of the two.

You may decide to implement peer review for the consolidation of the concepts learnt during the lesson. Each pair of students may exchange their work with their adjacent pair for feedback. The feedback must be written in pencil, along with the names of the reviewer students. The feedback may be in the form of some comments on whether they find the solution correct or some corrections they feel are necessary. The exercise books are to be submitted to you at the end of the lesson. The students' work, along with the feedback, will give you a clear idea about the level of understanding of the students.

Home Assignment: Research Work

Research the rules to play any one of the following games: snakes and ladders, tic-tac-toe or any other board game of their choice.

Please tell them that in the next class, they will need to discuss their findings with their partners, write the algorithm based on the discussion and draw a flowchart. The students must be informed that they may encounter more than one condition in the rules of the game they choose.

Peer Learning in Action

Peer learning is a type of collaborative learning pedagogy where, instead of depending solely on the teachers, the students learn from each other through the sharing of ideas, peer teaching as well and problem-solving. This pedagogy ensures active involvement of all the students and promotes the development of social skills.

Think–Pair–Share, peer tutoring, small group projects and peer review are some of the ways peer learning may be implemented.

Lesson 4: Introduction to Multiple Selection

Tools used: Think–Pair–Share, peer review.

Skills: Logical reasoning, critical thinking, collaboration, creativity, communication and social skills.

Teaching pedagogy/strategy: Collaborative peer/small group learning.

Collaborative Learning

- Promotes communication, understanding, HOTS.
- Aids longer retention, confidence and leadership skills.

Prerequisites

- Specify your expectations at the beginning of a term.
- Motivate and supervise during activity.
- Explain how to assess their peers (grading rubric)

Introduction to Multiple Decisions

The students must be somewhat confused as to how to implement multiple decisions in the algorithm or the flowchart for their chosen game (refer to the home assignment of Lesson 3). It will be a good idea to begin the class with the concept of multiple selections. How to use AND or how to avoid AND in certain circumstances may be explained at this stage.

Class Demonstration

I find it easier to explain the use of the AND operator by selecting one problem and showing the benefit of conjunction over multiple conditions by letting the students compare a flowchart implementing 'AND' and the other without it.

Example 1: Input three numbers and find out the largest.

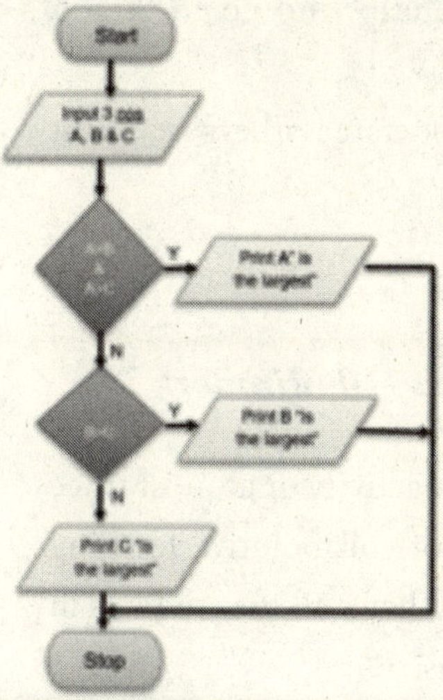

Conditions using AND

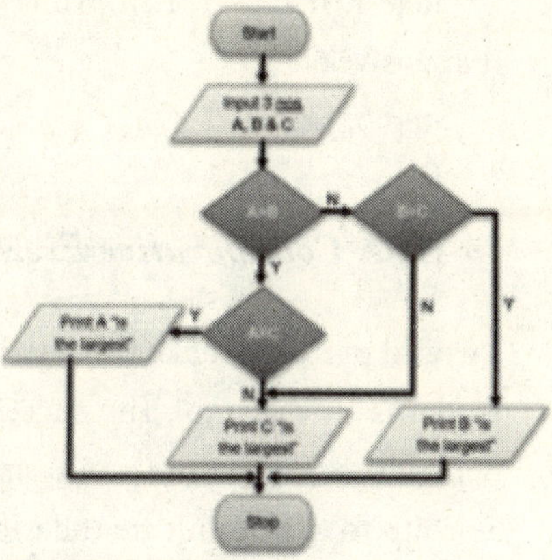

Conditions without using AND

Note: You may point out at this stage the importance of connecting the flow lines at the right place, and also let the students understand how a misplaced flow line can entirely change the logic of a program.

Example 2: Input the cost of a bar of chocolate. If the price is between 10–20, print 'Cheap'; between 21–80, print 'Moderate'; otherwise, print 'Expensive'. Draw the flowchart without using AND.

An explanation may be given that in case of a range of values, we can avoid using AND by taking only the upper limit into consideration.

Algorithm:

Step 1. Start.

Step 2. Input the price (P) of a chocolate bar.

Step 3. If P<21, then print 'Cheap' and go to Step 5 (demonstrating branching).

Step 4. If P<81, then print 'Moderate'; otherwise, print 'Expensive'.

Step 5. Stop.

In-Class Collaborative Exercises (10 Minutes)

I would prefer to make this a paired activity or at most three students in a group. The success of collaborative learning depends mostly on the group size. Allows all the students in a group to communicate their ideas.

Please provide sheets to each group to complete the exercises so that they can submit their work at the end of the lesson.

Example 3: Study the algorithm for Example 2 carefully and state what the output of the algorithm will be if the price (P) of the chocolate bar is input as:

i. -2 or ii. 20.50

Do you think your algorithm has mistakes? If yes, can you think of any change(s) that can be incorporated in the algorithm to rectify the mistakes?

Example 4: Admission to the nursery section of a reputed school is based on whether the child is between three to four years of age AND whether the child can recite a nursery rhyme OR can complete a block puzzle.

Write an algorithm to input the age (A) of the child, recitation (R), the input for R can be either YES or NO and puzzle (P), the input for P also will be either YES or NO.

Peer Group Corrections (5 Minutes)

Allow the groups to exchange their work with the adjacent groups. The corrections or comments made by the critics must be in pencil to distinguish between the original work and corrections.

Teacher–Student Interaction Time (10 Minutes)

Time for you to call out at least two to three critique groups to discuss the answers written by their peer groups, the errors they identified and the solutions they suggested. The chosen groups may pick up any one exercise for discussion. After listening to their deliberations, it is time for you to sum up with your observations. The students must note down your feedback in their exercise books. Please try to appreciate the hard work of the students and try not to come out with a completely different solution unless it is necessary.

Home Assignment (Some Suggestions)

Some questions to help the students apply logical reasoning and critical thinking.

1. Draw the flowchart for Example 4, the algorithm for which has been done in class.
2. Write the algorithm and draw a flowchart to check whether a number (N) is positive or negative.
3. In the national football academy, players are being selected for the U18 team on the following basis:
   a. The player must be 15–18 years of age.
   b. Must have qualified in at least two U18 trials or must have a recommendation letter from a national-level football coach.

   Write an algorithm and draw a flowchart to input Age (A), Number of trials qualified(N), recommendation letter (L – the input value can be YES or NO) and depending on the condition, the output should be 'Selected for U18' or 'Rejected'.

Modelling and Scaffolding in Action

I feel modelling and scaffolding strategies make teaching complex topics like iteration far simpler. To teach iteration, we will use a three-level strategy: '**I do**' (modelling), '**We do**' (scaffolding through shared instruction and guided practice), and finally, '**You do**' (independent learning). It is also referred to as Gradual Release of Responsibility (GRR), which means that the responsibility of learning begins with a teacher and then is gradually shifted to the students.

In Chapter 3, I have explained Vygotsky's Zone of Proximal Development. ZPD implies that learning can improve drastically with the support of a 'More Knowledgeable Other' (the teacher or a peer who knows more). The ZPD of each student may vary; some need more help, and some may flourish with very little support. It is important to know the ZPD of the students in class, as it will help you decide upon the degree of scaffolding during the 'We do' phase.

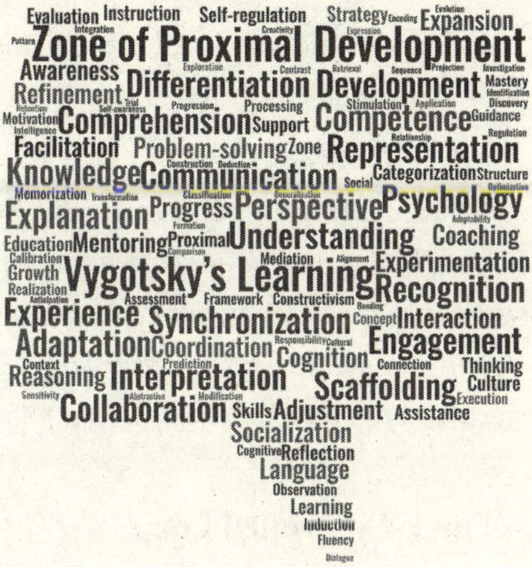

Please note that instead of cramming the modelling–scaffolding strategy in a single lesson, it would be wise to spread the process in several lessons for its success.

For teaching iteration, we will adopt the 'I do–We do–You do' strategy as follows:

Step 1. The teacher explains iteration with examples and work-outs, and the students listen and observe (I do, modelling).

Step 2. The teacher gives cues to the students and asks them to help during explanation (We do, shared instruction).

Step 3. The teacher forms pairs of students where each pair will have a 'More Knowledgeable Student' who will provide support while solving the problems the teacher gives. The task of the teacher would be to observe the groups' progress and facilitate the groups that need help (We do, guided practice).

Step 4. The students would try to solve problems on their own (You do, independent learning).

I have seen through my experience that even the best of the students take time to apply iterations correctly. I found the modelling and scaffolding technique quite useful for first-time learners. We have to utilize quite a number of lessons to drive home the concept. I often gave small exercises on looping as a brain teaser while teaching other topics till I found the students were confident.

Iteration – Entry-Controlled Loop

My experience says, students find it difficult and take more time to conceptualize iteration. This topic must be split into multiple lessons to enable students to build a strong foundation for the concept.

It is a good time to introduce a dry run to the students. A dry run is a problem-solving strategy used to trace the steps of an algorithm, a flowchart or a piece of code to determine the output. It can be used as a powerful tool to detect errors and perform necessary corrections.

Tools used: I do–We do–You do, dry run.

Skills: Logical reasoning, critical thinking, creativity, collaboration and communication.

Teaching pedagogy/strategy: Modelling and scaffolding.

> Providing students with models and worked examples can help them to learn to solve problems faster.
>
> – Rosenshine, 2012.

Introduction – I do

You may use simple real-life examples of looping/iteration to which the students can relate after introducing the topic. A couple of examples for you.

> Scaffolding is a teaching practice where the teacher removes guidance gradually to make students self-reliant.

Example 1: Neeta has created a list of 50 of her favourite songs on the Spotify music app. Once she plays the first song, the rest of the songs play automatically and stop only when the list of 50 songs is over. The process of playing songs repetitively for a certain number of times is iteration.

Example 2: Print 'I love my country' 50 times. Please let the students understand that either they type or write 'I love my country' 50 times, which can be quite time consuming, or they can write 'I love my country' once in a loop, which will run for 50 times to deliver the same result.

The students need to know that the two examples above are of finite entry-controlled loops.

They must also know that loops may also be infinite. You may ask the students whether they can provide examples of infinite loops, which never stop. Like, rotation and revolution of the earth, pumping of the heart and so on. Then you may share some.

Concept of a Counter in Finite Entry-Controlled Loops

Time to explain the concept of a counter and how it controls (control variable) finite loops. Please find below the algorithm and flowchart for Example 1.

Step 1. Start.

Step 2. Set counter to zero.

Step 3. If counter<50, then go to Step 4 otherwise go to Step 6.

Step 4. Play the next song in the list.

Step 5. Increment counter by one and go to Step 3.

Step 6. Stop.

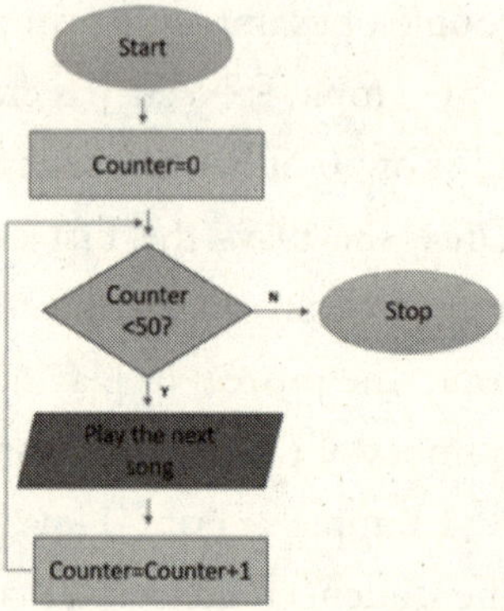

The students must understand that an entry-controlled loop is one where the body of the loop gets executed only if the condition stated at the head of the loop is true.

Since the number of iterations was known from before, an entry-controlled loop could be used in the above example. Please make the students aware that there are situations where exit-controlled loops are the better choice.

Please show them the dry run for the above example.

Counter	**Counter<50**	**Action**	**Output**
0	Yes	Counter=Counter+1	Next song
1	Yes	Counter=Counter+1	Next song
…	…	…	…
…	…	…	…
50	No	Stop	

Please ask the students to note the value of the counter at the end of the loop.

I have introduced the ***Action*** *column in the dry run to help the students relate to the algorithm. As you know, during the actual dry run, they need not use this column.*

Content – We Do

Time to implement Step 2 of our 'I do–We do–You do' strategy. Let us involve the students in the process of problem-solving with iteration. The best way to do it would be to read aloud the steps you are writing on the board and urge the students to help you complete the algorithm of a problem on iteration. You may need to provide cues as and when necessary.

I would start with simple problems of entry-controlled loops, like:

1. Write the algorithm to print the first 10 natural numbers. Please help the students understand that the function of a counter is not limited only to controlling a loop. In this case counter is going to be used to print a natural number.
2 Algorithm to print the even numbers between 50 and 10. (A hint must be given that the value of a counter may be increased or decreased by any number.)

I prefer doing the dry run of each problem along with the students to identify the More Knowledgeable Student.

Before implementing Step 3 of the 'I do–We do–You do' strategy, you need to quickly form the pairs as discussed earlier. Assign the pairs the following problem or something similar.

3. Algorithm to input 10 numbers and print whether they are positive or negative. (Students must understand that a loop may contain decision statements.)

The pairs must also complete the dry run of the problem with you being an observer and facilitator.

Summing Up

> According to Shaun Allison, the co-author of *Making Every Lesson Count,* the key importance of modelling is to help develop metacognition in the students.

Ask the students to call out the new terms that they have learnt during the lesson. You may list out the terms on the board. Pick students randomly and ask each of them to explain one concept they have learnt. Allow other students to rectify/add once you instruct them to do so. Class decorum must be maintained during the process of discussion.

I feel the students must be given a **brain break** after such a heavy-duty lesson. You may play some light music and let the students do some stretching while standing in their places.

I have talked about the importance of a brain break in Book 1.

Home Assignment – You Do

1. Write an algorithm and draw a flowchart to print negative numbers from -50 to -1.

2. Write an algorithm and draw the flowchart to print the series 2, 4, 6, 8… up to 40.

Iteration – Exit-Controlled Loop

Tools used: I do–We do–You do, Think–Pair–Share, dry run.

Skills: Logical reasoning, critical thinking, creativity, collaboration and communication.

Teaching pedagogy/strategy: Modelling and scaffolding, collaborative learning.

Introduction – I Do

The students must understand that an exit-controlled loop is one where the body of the loop is executed at least once, even if the condition is false, as the condition is checked after execution of the loop body.

The concept of an exit-controlled loop may be explained with the help of a real-life example.

Example 1: An ATM gives three chances to enter the correct PIN/password daily to a customer. If the customer enters the wrong PIN three times in a row, he/she is locked out for the day. Please explain to the students that the ATM software matches the PIN entered with the correct PIN stored in the database. If it is correct, it allows the customer to proceed with banking transactions; otherwise, the same process of PIN verification is repeated three times.

Example 2: Write an algorithm to input and print 10 positive numbers (N). Do not print anything if the number is negative.

Algorithm and flowchart for Example 1:

Step 1. Start.
Step 2. Set counter to 0.
Step 3. Enter ATM pin.
Step 4. If pin is correct go to Step 5 otherwise go to Step 6.
Step 5. Allow banking transaction and stop.
Step 6. Display 'Incorrect pin'.
Step 7. Increment counter by one.
Step 8. If counter<3 then go to Step 3 otherwise display 'You are locked out for the day'.
Step 9. Stop.

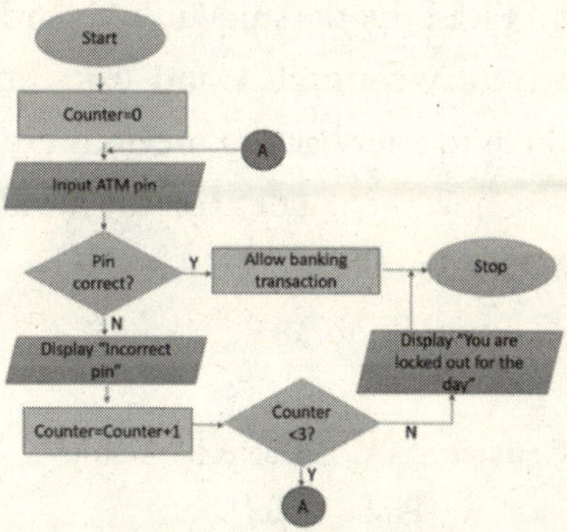

Please explain the purpose of using connectors in the flowchart to the students.

The students must understand why using an exit-controlled loop is the best choice for the above problem. The following explanation may suffice.

We know that the user gets three chances to input the correct PIN. The user may input the correct PIN at the first attempt or may require up to three attempts. This makes it necessary to input the PIN within a loop. However, the loop must stop once the correct pin is entered. That is why it is essential to check the PIN at the beginning of the loop.

Please ask the students to identify any difference between an entry-controlled and exit-controlled loop, and allow them to refer back to previous exercises.

Show them a dry run for the above exercise.

Input 1: 1234

Input 2: 3670

Counter	ATM Pin	Correct Pin?	Action	Counter<3?	Output
0	1234	No	Counter= Counter+1		Incorrect pin
1			Allow pin input	Yes	
1	3670	Yes	Allow banking transaction		

Algorithm and flowchart for Input 2:

Step 1. Start.
Step 2. Counter=0.
Step 3. Input a number, N.
Step 4. If N>0 then print N and increase Counter by 1.
Step 5. If Counter <10 then go to Step 3.
Step 6. Stop.

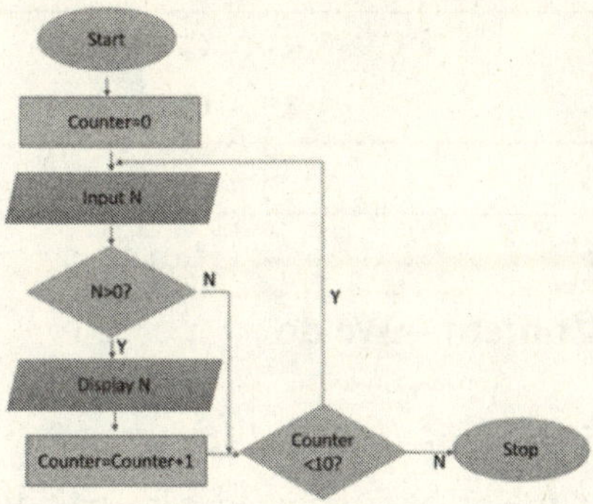

Please point out to the students that the flow of the control is going to Step 5 irrespective of N being positive or negative. However, since Counter is increasing only when N is positive, the loop will continue until 10 positive numbers have been input.

Dry run for the above algorithm:

Counter	N	N>0?	Action	Counter<10?	Output
0	12	Yes	Counter= Counter+1		12
1	67	Yes	Counter= Counter+1	Yes	67

2	-8	No	-	Yes	-
2	-90	No	-	Yes	-
...	....	...	....	....	....
2	45	Yes	Counter= Counter+1	Yes	45
3	...	...	.....	...	...

Content – We do

Since exit-controlled loops require greater understanding, it might be a good idea to pair up students to solve the problems you would assign to them.

For example, write an algorithm to input a number and print whether it is odd or even. The process must stop if the number entered is zero.

- Ask the students whether they find the need for a counter here to control the loop.

Feedback Time

Please encourage a few pairs of students to share their solution on the board. If the solution offered by a pair is incorrect, ask other pairs to share theirs. Please do not offer the correct solution unless it is necessary.

Home Assignment – You Do

Please cut down on some of the earlier exercises, if necessary, to accommodate at least one independent learning exercise in class. It would give you an idea of the overall learning of the students. Some suggested exercises for you.

1. Draw the flowchart, and do the dry run to input a number and print whether it is odd or even. The process must continue if the user enters their choice as 'yes'. Otherwise, the process must stop.
2. Algorithm, flowchart and dry run to input a number N and print whether it is a perfect number or not. A perfect number is equal to the sum of its factors. For example, 6=1+2+3, 28=1+2+4+7+14. So, 6 and 28 are perfect numbers. [Hint: check if the counter is a factor; if yes, keep adding the value of the counter.]

Chapter 11

Constructivist Learning Theory, Experiential and Interdisciplinary Learning Theory

We have implemented CLT in many of our earlier lessons. CLT is a contemporary learning theory which has its roots in John Dewey's progressive education, Jean Piaget's cognitivism and Lev Vygotsky's Social Learning Theory. In this chapter, we are going to implement **Interdisciplinary Learning Theory** along with CLT. This theory was not the work of a single person. William H. Newell popularized and formalized the theory by providing a theoretical foundation and practical framework for interdisciplinary studies in 'A Theory of Interdisciplinary Studies'. This theory combines learning gained from different subjects and empowers students to address a problem from different perspectives. Such integration of multiple disciplines leads to holistic learning, builds problem-solving, critical thinking and collaboration skills.

We are going to use a **microlearning video** in this chapter to introduce the topic of computer viruses. Since the students are already aware of malicious software from their personal experiences, we will give them a **case study** and questions based on that to solve in the class. This can be a paired work. We will use a graphic organizer, **Concept Map**, to summarize the topics and the sub-topics learnt for a concise and structured coverage. We will use **storytelling** to make teaching more dramatic and enthralling.

We may implement experiential learning by conducting a reflection workshop while teaching the topic of cybercrime.

Cross-Curricular Project/Assignment Ideas

You may implement cross-curricular learning by collaborating with subjects like mathematics and English for projects or class assignments. It will require careful planning with the teachers of the subjects concerned at the beginning of a term/academic year. The students may collect data through survey forms in their locality and family to find out whether there have been incidents of **financial fraud**, **impersonation** or **virus attacks**. They may also collect information on the **antivirus software** being used, whether a **firewall** is being used by the respondents. Under yours and the mathematics teacher's guidance, the data thus collected may be fed into Excel sheets and used by the students to analyse, create graphs and interpret the demographic percentage being affected by malicious software, percentage of respondents aware of how to protect themselves and so on. Please involve the students in designing the data collection form with you as a facilitator. It will make the exercise more meaningful.

The English teacher may ask the students to write a **short story** on malicious programs or an **essay** on 'Which is the best way to protect children from cyberbullying' as an assignment.

Please share this document prepared by the Ministry of Home Affairs, Government of India, https://www.mha.gov.in/sites/default/files/CyberSafety_English_Web_03122018_0.pdf with the students before starting the topic, so that they can refer to this document before the topic begins.

Cyber Safety Handbook

Problem-Based Learning in Action

Topic: Computer Virus

This topic has been divided into three lessons implementing the strategies mentioned above: ***threats to computers, viruses and their types and symptoms of infection and sources of viruses.***

Problem-based learning is a type of active learning where students are given some real-life scenarios to solve. It is a learning method where the teacher takes a back seat as a facilitator and involves students to analyse a real-life problem through critical thinking, collaboration and practical knowledge.

Tools used: Case study, concept map.

Skills: Information literacy, media literacy, technology literacy, decision-making, problem-solving.

Teaching pedagogy/strategy: Active learning, microlearning video, case study.

Introduction Through a Microlearning Video

You may decide to begin the class by showing a small video on computer viruses, their origin and history, which includes the story of the first-ever virus, **Creeper**, and the first-ever antivirus, **Reaper**.

VIRUS:

Vital **I**nformation **R**esources **U**nder **S**iege

I have used invideo.ai to create this video from the website's stock and uploaded it to my channel. The link is: https://youtu.be/QfDyynqI46U. Although a little lengthy (6:08 minutes), this video covers almost every aspect of the history of the virus.

History of Computer Virus

If you want, you may also use this time as a storytelling session by sharing dramatic stories about damages caused by malware.

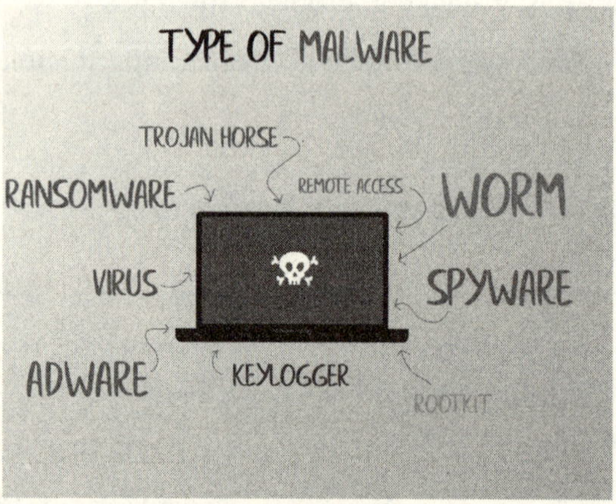

Types of Malware

Content

Now that the students have watched the video or listened to your story, you may begin by asking the students to express their views on the following:

1. Why do they think the viruses are created?
2. Who creates a virus and why?

You may utilize three to five minutes of your time for this interactive Q&A session.

You may now use a case study on the ILOVEYOU worm, the reference for which is shared at the end in Annexure 1. Let this be a paired work. Take printouts of the case study before the class and share a copy with each pair. Give the students five minutes to read. Display questions related to the topic on the whiteboard or write on the blackboard. Another five minutes will be required to answer.

Some suggested questions for you.

1. Is ILOVEYOU a virus or a worm?
2. How was it transmitted?
3. How did it infect a user's computer?
4. What threat did it pose?
5. How would you protect your computer from such malware?

You may now use a concept map to teach types of malware, spreading techniques, effects, prevention methods, as well as detection and removal methods. I have created a sample concept map in PowerPoint for you.

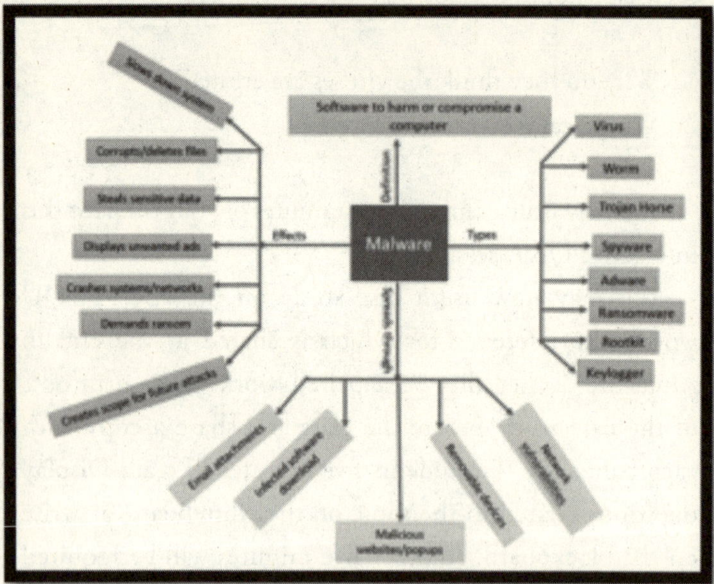

A Concept Map on Malware

You may ask the students to expand the above concept map by adding the features of each type of malware as a home assignment. The best way to do it would be to share two samples with them as below.

Although they may seem similar(they are both visual organization tools), there are certain differences in the way concept maps and mind maps are used.

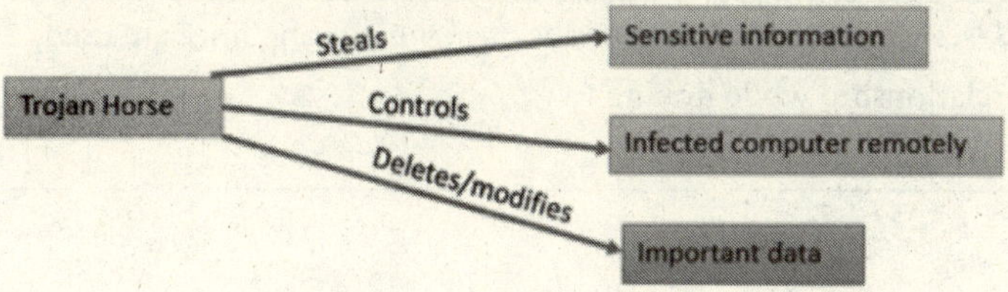

Concept Map Extension for Trojan Horse

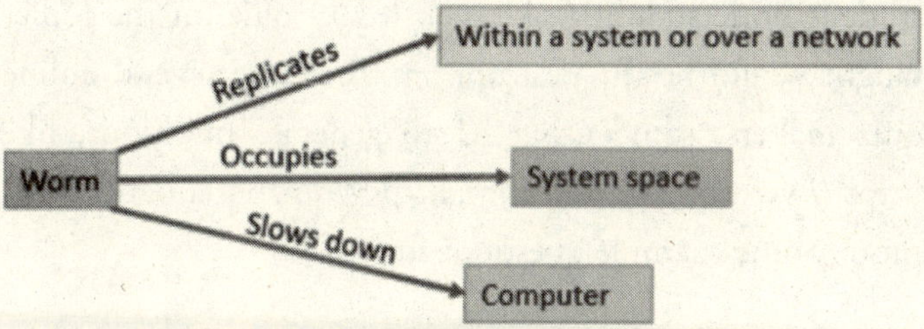

Concept Map Extension for Worm

The main differences between a concept map and a mind map are:

Concept Map	Mind Map
Contains main concept and sub-concepts in a hierarchical fashion.	Contains a central idea and branches and are usually arranged radially.
It is used to organize complex information in a structured manner for better understanding.	Mainly used for creative idea generation through brainstorming, taking notes.

Uses words/phrases to describe relationship while linking concepts and sub-concepts	Only linking lines are used.

Summing Up – Formative Assessment

To sum up, you may use formative assessment to judge student understanding. A quick MCQ quiz on the topics taught would be the best option. There are several online quiz makers, some using AI to generate questions, like https://www.quiz-maker.com, https://quizbot.ai/ and many more. Some example questions for you:

1. Damages to the computer systems due to a natural calamity like an earthquake are
   a) Intentional threat b) Accidental threat
2. A small piece of malicious software that can replicate itself and occupy system space
   a) Virus b) Worm c) Trojan
3. A malware that disguises itself as a useful program and then modifies or deletes system resources
   a) Email virus b) Trojan horse c) Spyware
4. A small program that displays unsolicited advertisements as a pop-up or banner, and clicking on which installs a virus into the system
   a) Worm b) Adware c) Spyware

5. A program that gets installed on a computer or mobile device without the user's knowledge and passes sensitive information to some outside source
   a) Spyware b) Trojan horse c) Virus

Home Assignment

1. It would be an interesting exercise to ask the students to make a scrapbook page(s) in their homework exercise book and paste information about any five recent malware or activities that have threatened computer systems in recent times. They must mention the source (the name of the website/newspaper and the date on which it was published) from which they have collected the information.
2. What is two-factor authentication? (They may ask their parents or search the internet.)
3. Encryption is the process of converting data into an unreadable form while it is being sent, and decryption is the process of unscrambling the unreadable data into a readable form. The students must cite two situations when data encryption may be necessary.
4. Finally, the students need to learn about different types of cybercrimes from their textbook/web and be ready for fun activities in the next class.

Storytelling and Inquiry-Based Pedagogy in Action

Storytelling pedagogy can be a powerful tool to teach cybersecurity to middle schoolers. Instead of using dry theoretical topics from the textbook, you can create realistic scenarios using proper narratives to make students understand the purpose of safe cybersecurity practices and the consequences one has to face failing to do so.

One has to be careful about the premise of the story being told, avoid using complicated jargon and use scenarios the students can relate to. Finally, a story with simple but engaging language and tone can do wonders.

In this lesson, we will involve the students in research work to learn about certain topics which will not be taught in class. It is an **inquiry-based approach** that encourages the students to question, explore, investigate and find answers through research.

Antivirus Software, Firewall, Cybercrime and Hackers and Crackers

Inquisitive students find it interesting when the algorithm behind a software is shared. Introducing students to virus simulators will give them a real feel for the role of hackers and crackers. For teaching about computer viruses, it is not essential to teach each and every concept in the classroom. The students may research some topics to learn about them.

Tools used: Storytelling, algorithm, virus simulator, research work.

Skills: Information literacy, media literacy, technology literacy, decision making, problem solving, social skill.

Teaching pedagogy/strategy: Storytelling, inquiry-based learning.

Introduction to Antivirus and Firewall (5–7 Minutes)

A quick run-through of antivirus software, how it works and some examples, which I am sure the students will be able to provide, can set the tone for the lesson.

Please find below an algorithm for the working principle of an Antivirus program, which could be used to explain the working mechanism of an antivirus to the students.

Step 1. Antivirus scans any new file that enters the computer. It also regularly scans existing files on the device for suspicious activity.

Step 2. If it finds anything suspicious, it matches the suspicious code with its database of viruses.

Step 3. If a match is found, it either quarantines or deletes the file; otherwise, it sends information about the new threat to the vendor.

Step 4. The vendor creates new code to combat a new virus, and the antivirus gets updated regularly.

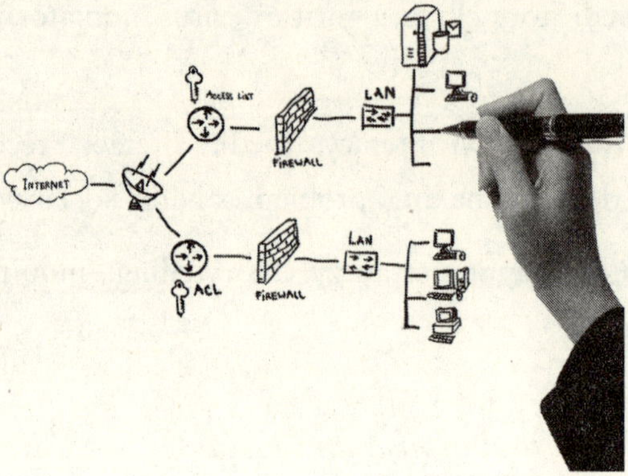

How Does a Firewall Work?

A **firewall** is a hardware device or software which filters out harmful content from entering a computer system or network. An **antivirus** is a software which detects and removes malware from a computer.

The above diagram may be used to explain the working principle of a firewall.

Storytelling Session

Time to get into an interactive session on the types of cybercrimes. I am sure the students will be only too eager to share their personal experiences without knowing the exact technical terms. You need to reinforce with your inputs on the stories they told and share the technical terms with them.

From the list of cybercrimes – phishing, ransomware, cyberbullying, cyberstalking, financial fraud, spamming, identity theft, e-commerce fraud, software piracy and so on – the students may have covered quite a few. You may decide to share short stories on some of the remaining crimes, which will have a lasting impact on the students. ChatGPT gives you a lot of story ideas.

Home Assignment

Please ask the students to **play** https://hacker-simulator.com/ and https://pranx.com/hacker/ online to get a feel of hacking. These two simulators have been designed to raise awareness about computer security. The students must write a small report on the features and which one they prefer.

Research about the following terms: netiquette, copyright infringement, plagiarism, flame war, trolling, digital footprint and the difference between an electronic and digital signature. Note down the concepts that you did not understand.

Active and Collaborative Learning Using Differentiation

You may have noticed that most of the lessons are designed based on active learning. It has been observed that active learning leads to increased student involvement, promotes a dynamic learning environment, involves better understanding and retention, leading to enhanced learning outcome. Moreover, it fosters critical thinking, problem-solving as well as analytical skills, which are essential for a twenty-first century learner.

In the earlier lessons. I have suggested paired learning in most cases. However, the objective of this lesson is collaboration in larger groups to cultivate leadership quality, mutual understanding, team spirit and to enable students of varied learning styles to work together to the best of their abilities.

This lesson is your opportunity to implement Howard Gardner's theory of **Multiple Intelligences (MI)** through differentiation in your classroom. Gardner talked about intelligence as a combination of eight distinct abilities – **linguistic** (has good command over language); **logical–mathematical** (capable of thinking and acting logically and good at mathematics); **spatial** (the ability to visualize and modify images mentally and understand the spatial relationship between objects); **musical**; **bodily–kinaesthetic** (good at dance, acting, craft making, athletics, interpersonal, intrapersonal); and **naturalistic** (connected to nature and environment). To apply this theory, you need to practice differentiation, a learning strategy that caters to the diverse requirements of the students. Differentiation demands that you understand the characteristics of each type of intelligence, assess the intelligence of your students, group them according to their intelligence type and conceive diverse activities based on each group's abilities.

I always made it a practice to consult the class teacher to know the students better. The dossier of the children also gave me ideas about their preferences.

GARDNER'S THEORY OF MULTIPLE INTELLIGENCES

In-Class Project Work

Tools used: Small-group (four to five students) activity.

Skills: Information literacy, media literacy, technology literacy, leadership, decision-making, problem-solving, social skill, social sensitivity, social and emotional intelligence.

Teaching pedagogy/strategy: Active learning, collaborative learning, differentiation.

Planning and Preparation

Plan to divide the class into small groups of four to five students following the theory of MI. Prepare paper chits, each containing the name of a cybercrime/threat or criminal (hacker/cracker). Please carry chart papers, sketch pens, coloured tapes, double-sided tapes/cello tapes/board pins to the class.

The students must be informed about the groups they belong to before the lesson. The seating arrangement of the class must be shuffled to create space for the groups. This must be ready before the lesson begins to save time.

I used to inform the class teacher and the class monitors at least a week prior to the activity. So, by the time I entered, the seating arrangement would be ready.

Instructions to the Groups

Each group needs to pick up a chit. They can create a poster/skit/doodle/song/poetry/presentation, or any other means to create awareness on the topic they picked and how to take precautions. They may use their textbooks or other resources to gather information. They can ask for chart paper and sketch pens. The groups must get 30 minutes to create their first draft. They do not need to be perfect; their ideas, approach and content will matter. The activity needs to be graded.

Content Creation by the Groups (30 Minutes)

It is time for active learning through collaboration. You, as a facilitator, must move from group to group to oversee the planning of the groups, guide them if they are stuck. At the end of 30 minutes, the groups submit their work to you for a quick look. Please return their work for further modifications and inform the groups that they have to present their creation in the next class. Each group will be provided three minutes to present their creation. The groups who have created skits must not completely change their theme; however, they may add/delete some dialogue.

Grading Rubric for Presentation on Cybercrime

Total points = 30	**Meets the Criteria 100 Per Cent (5)**	**Meets the Criteria Partially (3)**	**Does not Meet any Criteria (1)**
All the members clearly understand the topic			
Satisfactory content development			
Presentation is visually appealing and complete			
All members have participated in content creation			

All members have participated in presentation
Satisfactory Q&A session

Please invite other teachers and the academic heads during the presentation. This will boost the enthusiasm of the students. Invite audience questions. Please request someone to document the activities by clicking pictures and videos while you are busy grading them.

Blogging with the Differentiation Technique

In the earlier section, 11.3, we implemented MI with differentiation. In this part, we will try to implement differentiation while teaching blogging, taking student interest, learning styles and readiness into consideration. This strategy promotes inclusion, gives freedom of choice to the students and allows students to reach their potential. The objective will

Why a Blog?

To express thoughts and views with others and receive feedback.

To express thoughts and views with others and receive feedback.

Why a Blog?

To express thoughts and views with others and receive feedback.

be to involve all the students of the class in the process of learning by tailoring content suitable for each learner.

We will use differentiation by content, process, learning environment and product.

Differentiation by content means what the students will learn.

Differentiation by process means how the students will learn.

Differentiation by environment means with whom the students will learn and create.

Differentiation by product means what the students will create to demonstrate their learning.

Tools used: Free and safe blogging sites suitable for kids like **Kidblog**, **Edublogs** or a professional blogging platform like **WordPress.com** for the advanced learners. For creating video blogs, **Microsoft Movie Maker** or **Canva** may be used. Kidblog also supports audio blogs. The students may use **Google Docs** for collaborative editing of the blog's content.

Skills: Technology literacy, critical thinking, creativity, communication, collaboration, research.

Teaching pedagogy/strategy: Visual and interactive learning, learning by differentiation.

Introduction

The lesson may begin with an interactive Q&A on students' current knowledge of blogs and their types. Please ask the students whether they can point out the differences between a website and a blog.

> **Blog vs Website**
>
> Blogs share personal opinions or perspectives whereas a website shares information about an entity, business or organization.

It would be a good idea to show the students some blogs created by other middle schoolers in India. It would give them a fair idea about the structure, look and content of a blog. I found some interesting blogs on https://beyondthebox.in/

After showing a blog, please encourage the students to share their opinions about the blog. A few blog links for your perusal. Please make the session interactive, and add your feedback as well.

https://thethoughtsexpress.blogspot.com/

https://kidsethics.com/

https://panyabhathijaa.wixsite.com/website

Comment: redundant because the heading states the same.

Things Students Must Keep in Mind Before Creating a Blog:

1. The blog must be on a topic that interests you, such as food, travel, technology, games or social awareness.
2. The name of the blog must be interesting.
3. The format of writing should be informal and conversational.
4. The target audience must be kept in mind during writing.

5. Relevant images, videos, preferably clicked personally, must be uploaded to make the blog look eye-catching.
6. New posts must be added at a regular interval.
7. The first blog may contain a short introduction of the blogger, the reason for creating the blog and what people can expect out of the blog.

Note for the students: Never copy and paste from other blogs or websites. You may quote with proper acknowledgement of the source.

Choosing a Platform

Initially, advise students to choose a free platform which offers free templates. Once they become good at it, they may upgrade to have their domain and Content Management System (CMS). WordPress.com has a detailed tutorial for beginners. You may share the link with your students: https://wordpress.com/support/tutorials/five-step-blog-setup/

Differentiation by Content

This strategy will be perfect as the **introductory lesson,** allowing you to identify students based on their abilities. Please give them the freedom to work alone, in pairs or small groups of three or four. It is preferable to take the students to the lab, so that they can conduct research as well as other work related to blog creation.

Please share a list of creative/informative/opinion-based topics to choose from. Allow them to create audio/video/text-based blogs according to their abilities and inclinations.

When I first used differentiation, it seemed a little chaotic, as some students were moving around the lab to form teams, whereas others were discussing excitedly about the topic they would choose. With a little intervention from my end, the students settled down and carried on with their business. Only the initial few minutes are challenging.

Absolute beginners, who have no clue as to how to create a blog, may decide upon a topic and write a paragraph in MS Word or Google Docs without getting much into the structure of a blog.

Students at the **intermediate level**, who have a fair idea about blogs, may decide upon a topic and write the content in MS Word or Google Docs following a structure – title, introduction, body and conclusion. They may even plan the content of an audio or video blog.

Advanced students, who know how to create a blog and have published some already, may research how to do **guest blogging**, **niche blogging** and learn the basics of **Search Engine Optimization (SEO)** to make their blogs more visible.

Differentiation by Process

This strategy will require about two to three lessons till the time the blog gets created. The idea is to make the students learn the same thing using different methods/processes, depending upon the interest, level of expertise and learning styles. The process of blog creation may be segregated into three levels – beginner, intermediate and advanced.

Levels	For Whom	The Process
Level 1	Beginners or the ones who require help.	Will work with teacher/peer support. They may be provided with a blog template and some phrases to begin each section of the template.
Level 2	Intermediate level, for visual or auditory learners, ones who possess oratory skills or are creative.	Visual learners may create a blog having images, videos or infographics or a vlog. These visual components must preferably be their own creations. Auditory learners may record a summary of their blog and then go on to listen to it and expand it into a textual blog. A student with oratory skills may create an audio blog which is a combination of audio and written content.

		A creative student may combine all the features mentioned above to create a blog.
Level 3	Advanced learners	An advanced learner can take blogging to the next level by incorporating guest blogging, niche blogging along with some SEO.

A Sample Template for Blog Creation

Title of the blog	It must be something catchy, related to the theme.
Purpose of the blog	It could be informative/entertainment/concern over some issue.
Introduction	A short paragraph on why are you writing this blog.
Body	The description of the topic.
Conclusion	It must be an interesting ending with key takeaways or a thought-provoking question for the readers.
Layout	Create a layout on paper/PowerPoint and decide upon images to use and links of other blogs to insert (if required).

Differentiation by Product

This differentiation is created based on the format of the blog. The students may choose to create a 1) Text blog, 2) Photo blog, 3) Comic strip blog, 4) Audio blog or 5) Video blog. The above blog template may be useful for any format that the students use.

Differentiation by Environment

This means where and how the students would like to work. They may want to work alone, in pairs or small groups. Some may like a quiet corner of the lab to ideate, some may use the computer to research and others may like to brainstorm within their groups. With your vigilance and intervention, the entire process will be like a dream.

Suggested Grading Rubric

Assessment Criteria	Did Not Meet Expectation (5 points)	Met Expectation (5 points)	Exceeded Expectation (5 points)
Choice of topic			
Use of expression			
Use of language			
Use of visuals			
Audience engagement			

Chapter 12

Structure–Process–Outcome Theory and Social Interdependence Theory

In this chapter, we will implement cooperative learning to teach podcasting. **Cooperative learning** is a teaching method where students learn through cooperation. In this approach, students with mixed abilities can be grouped to achieve a shared goal. This strategy helps individual students to improve their learning as well as the learning of other group members.

According to Johnson and Johnson, cooperative learning has its roots in theories of **Structure–Process–Outcome (SPO)** and **Social Interdependence**. SPO theory posits that the quality of learning is measured on three interdependent factors – **structure** (classroom resources like curriculum plan, teaching resources, space, etc.), **process** (classroom teaching, class activities, assessments) and **outcome** (marks on assessment, grades on projects). Changes in each of these factors can affect the quality of learning.

Social Interdependence Theory states that the way goals are structured in a group affects how people interact – and those interactions affect outcomes. This means that when the students in a group help and support each other, through positive interdependence, they succeed in making their common goal a reality.

Jigsaw Learning Strategy in Action

Jigsaw learning strategy is a unique cooperative learning method which makes the students in a group support and learn from each other through interdependence and are motivated

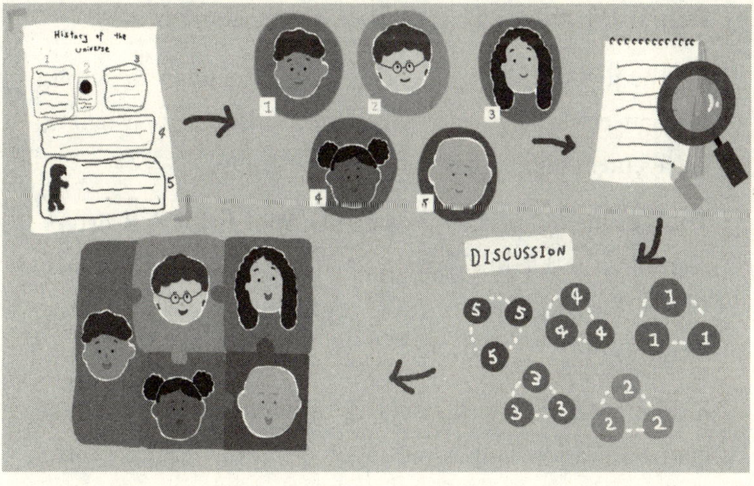

to work together to fulfil a shared goal. Interdependence makes each student in a group an active learner.

The above diagram clearly explains the concept of Jigsaw learning.

Step 1. A task is divided into many sub-tasks.

Step 2. The students of the class are grouped based on mixed abilities, and each group is assigned a sub-task.

Step 3. Members of each group research individually on the topic assigned and then get back to their group members to brainstorm and come to a common understanding.

Step 4. All the groups get together like the pieces of a jigsaw, and one member of each group shares the findings of the group.

Step 5. The groups work to create the final product.

The jigsaw technique makes each student in the group play an essential part of the whole, encourages listening, engagement and empathy within the group.

Tools used: Free podcasting sites like **Spotify for Podcasters**, recording and editing apps like **Audacity** or **Riverside**, **Canva** for cover art design, **Google Docs** for collaborative script writing.

Skills: Technology literacy, critical thinking, creativity, communication, collaboration, cooperation, research, social skills.

Teaching pedagogy/strategy: Jigsaw strategy, a form of cooperative learning and interdisciplinary learning.

Introduction

What is Podcasting?

It is a series of digital audio or video files uploaded on the web that may be downloaded on any device for listening or viewing at a convenient time. Usually, the contents of podcasts are interviews, game or movie reviews, inspiring talk on social and global issues and so on.

> **Why Podcast?**
>
> It is an interesting way to share information, your views as well as inspire people. A good podcast helps you to engage your audience.
>
> It is meant for people who prefer listening over reading.

Please show the students some podcasts created by students. You may find this link useful: https://www.kqed.org/mindshift/53791/8-student-made-podcasts-that-made-us-smile Yet another one for your use, https://www.brainson.org/episode/2018/12/25/earthrise-photo-solar-system

After playing a podcast, ask for opinions from the students. Some suggestions for you:

QR Code for Link 1: Student-made podcasts that made us smile

QR Code for Link 2: Earthrise: The picture of our planet that changed the world

i. Did you find the topic interesting?
ii. How was the cover art?
iii. How was the quality of the recording?
iv. How was the content?

Podcasting Using the Jigsaw Technique

Step 1. Share a few topics of a podcast – like interviewing your class teacher, about the school library, a conversation between a few cartoon characters from the animated comedy, *Ice Age*, on global warming, a storytelling session and so on.

Step 2. Finalize the topic through an **opinion poll** (may be through a raise of hands).

Step 3. Divide the class into four **podcast expert groups** – script writers, voices of the podcast, the techies and the designers. Each group must comprise students with diverse abilities. All the groups must get the opportunity to research.

- **Script writers**: This group will develop the storyline and the characters. They will then create a script with dialogues and roles for emcees and narrators. It will require students with linguistic abilities. The students must consult with their English teacher to get guidance and feedback.
- **Voices of the podcast**: These students will lend their voices for different roles, including emcees and narrators. Most students must possess a clear accent, diction and voice modulation capabilities. This group must train with the drama teacher and the music teacher with their scripts and dialogues.
- **The Techies**: This team will decide upon the software to be used. Will perform the recording and editing tasks. They must consult with you to identify the best-fit software and sit with you to learn to use the software.

- **The Designers:** This team will design the podcast cover and other props (like background images) required for the podcast. They will also select the background score(s) for the podcast. This team must consult with their art teacher and music teacher on their cover art design and choice of music.

Step 4. Select one mature student as the **group leader,** who will be responsible for maintaining cohesion within the group and communicating with other group leaders as and when necessary.

Step 5. Ensure that each student gets to play a part in the group. For example, the script must not be written by just one student. Each student of the group must be assigned a character or a scene to develop. They will then get together to complete the whole script.

Step 6. Students must get ample time to prepare themselves before getting to produce the podcast. Ideally, this could become a summer project with preparations beginning at least a couple of weeks before.

Step 7. During the initial preparation phase, move from group to group during your lesson to know about the hurdles they are facing and seek help from the concerned teachers.

Step 8. Ensure that the podcast recording is done in school. That will give you and the other teachers responsible a chance to see how the finished product is made.

Step 9. You may organize an assembly for Grade 8 where the students may present their podcasts and take questions from the audience. It will be nice if other teachers and the administrators are present.

Gadgets Required

They may begin with what they already have, like a smartphone, a laptop with a webcam and a microphone and a tablet. Gradually, as they master the art and become genuinely interested, they may invest in better quality gadgets.

Chapter 13

Constructivism and Cooperative Learning Theory

Planning must be done right at the beginning of the session to invite a **resource person** from the **cybercrime cell of the local police** or a **cybersecurity expert** to interact with the students. The best time to hold the session would be after the topic is over. This is a topic pertinent to all the students of the middle school. It would be a good idea to involve the teachers and parents in this programme.

In this chapter, we are trying to implement **case-based learning (CBL)** and **reciprocal questioning** to teach computer ethics, cyber law and its importance, backup and restore.

CBL stems from cognitivism. It engages students in the analysis of real-life scenarios. There is a distinct difference between CBL and PBL. In CBL, students apply existing knowledge to analyse a real-life scenario. In PBL, students acquire new knowledge while analysing a real-life scenario.

I found **reciprocal questioning** to be an interesting strategy to build upon the questioning, clarifying, summarizing and prediction skills of the students. It is a cooperative learning strategy where the students learn some concepts before the lesson and ask questions to the teacher. These questions could be on **fuzzy points** or questions pertaining to the topic. The teacher must be ready to answer without taking the help of any reference materials.

> **Fuzzy point** is a topic/concept which the students could not grasp or found confusing during self-learning.

Reciprocal Questioning and Case-Based Learning in Action

Topics: Computer Ethics, cyber law and its importance, backup and restore

> **Reciprocal questioning** is a cooperative learning strategy where the students and the teacher question each other to gain knowledge on a particular topic.

Preparations for class: The students must research the terms – trolling/online defamation, cyberbullying, intellectual property rights, copyright infringement, digital footprint, data privacy and protection, plagiarism, cybercrime, responsible online behaviour, importance of backup and restore, etc., before the class and prepare questions to ask the teacher.

Tools used: Fuzzy point, reciprocal questioning.

Skills: Information literacy, media literacy, technology literacy, questioning, clarification, summarization and prediction.

Teaching pedagogy/strategy: Active learning, case-based learning, cooperative learning.

Reciprocal Questioning Time

It would be a good idea to ask the students to form small groups of three to four students. Give each group about three to four minutes to look into their resources, consult with each other and frame one or two questions for you.

> **Reciprocal teaching** is best represented as a dialogue between teachers and students in which participants take turns assuming the role of teacher.
>
> – Annemarie Sullivan Palincsar

At times, I came across questions for which I did not have ready answers. I had to be candid and told them that I would get back with the answers in the next class, or asked them to give me the answer. I always appreciated their effort in smart questioning.

The groups may take turns in the entire process of reciprocal questioning.

When it is your turn to question the students, some questions from your end could be:

1. What does it mean to chat in capital letters?
2. Why do we use abbreviations during chatting?
3. A famous actor gets trolled for insensitive comments made by him on social media. What is trolling?
5. What is copying someone's work as your own called?
6. Does it violate the copyright act?
7. Does your browser keep track of your digital footprint?
8. Difference between digital signature and electronic signature. An electronic signature is the digital form of a handwritten signature, which may not be recognized legally in all kinds of transactions, whereas a digital signature is legally verified and secure signature that is certified by a trusted service provider.

Success Key for Reciprocal Questioning Strategy:

1. **Appreciate** the effort of the groups who have formulated pertinent and intelligent questions.
2. **Encourage** the groups whose question formulation was not up to the mark.
3. **Modify** questions asked by the groups (do not discard) if possible, and then **answer**.

4. Allow to **reframe** questions, to the groups whose questions were not up to the mark.

Case-Based Learning Time

Use this part of the lesson to gauge the understanding of the students on **ethics**, **cyber law**, its importance and the need for **backup** and **restore** with the help of real-life cases. You may ask the students to i) Think critically, ii) Decide whether each case is ethical or unethical and iii) What would they do and write their answers in their exercise books.

Case 1: Someone posted a funny picture of your friend on the class WhatsApp group. Your friend was completely unaware of it.

Case 2: Nadia copied a block of text from a website and used it to complete her project work without acknowledging the website.

Case 3: Someone in your class saw you typing your Gmail password when you were working on a computer in the library. Your classmate logged in to your Gmail account using your password and sent random emails to your other classmates as a prank.

Case 4: You have posted a few pictures of the class picnic on Facebook. A classmate is being teased in the comments by some other friends. You are not part of it, but you see it happening.

Case 5: You deleted a shared file by mistake from Google Drive, but did not report it to anyone.

Case 6: You received an email with a link promising unlimited free mobile data. It looks fake, but you're curious.

Case 7: Your friend hacked into the school portal and found the question papers for the final term. The friend is sharing them with his close friends, including you.

Case 8: You overheard that some of your friends use AI tools to do their homework and never get caught. They suggested you do the same.

Case 9: You usually keep three copies of all important files, one in your computer's hard disk, one in a flash drive and another on Google Drive. You forgot to back up the latest file on Google Drive. Your computer has crashed, and the flash drive is corrupted.

Case 10: You worked hard and submitted your history project on time. A few days later, your history teacher reprimanded you, saying that you had copied from another classmate.

Please discuss **ethical hacking**. This is the right time for them to understand that **plagiarism** is illegal. Explain to them the need for **citations** while borrowing information from the web. Explain to them the term **netiquette**.

Summing Up

Please ask the small groups to discuss among themselves and create rules for **'Responsible Online Behaviour'**.

Please provide them with A4-sized sheets on which they will create their rule list.

Chapter 14

Constructivism, Experiential Learning and Self-Determination and Flow Theory

In this chapter, we are going to use **gamification** to teach the internet and online surfing concepts. I find no better way to teach this chapter than this strategy. Gamification stems from constructivism, experiential learning, self-determination and flow theory. **Self-determination** is a motivational theory that ensures better student engagement and learning outcomes when the students have choices, feel more capable and can relate to their peers and the concepts being taught. **Flow Theory** suggests that educators can guarantee augmented student motivation, engagement and learning outcomes by creating learning experiences that support flow, a state which makes the students totally engrossed in an activity, losing track of time.

Gamification in Action

Topics: Networks, internet, intranet, websites, web browsers, opening of web pages and websites, search engine.

Tools used: Gamification, classification chart, mind map.

Skills: Technology literacy, collaboration, questioning, clarification, summarization, prediction.

Teaching pedagogy/strategy: Active learning/experiential learning.

Introduction

Eliciting Prior Knowledge

You may decide to begin the lesson with a Q&A session to find out the level of understanding the students have of the topics. Some sample questions which you may ask:

1. You can easily share files between the computers, tabs, smartphones at your home. What makes it possible?
2. What is the internet or WWW?
3. What is Wi-Fi?
5. Does Bluetooth form a network?
6. What is a mobile hotspot used for?
7. Where do you get free Wi-Fi hotspots in public areas?
8. What is broadband?

Summarize and reflect on the session with the students, offer feedback and rectify misconceptions.

Content

By now, the students have acquired the basic concept of networking and some related jargon. The stage is set to delve deeper into the topic network.

Types of Networks

Please share a classification chart on the type of networks based on the area covered, along with an example for each.

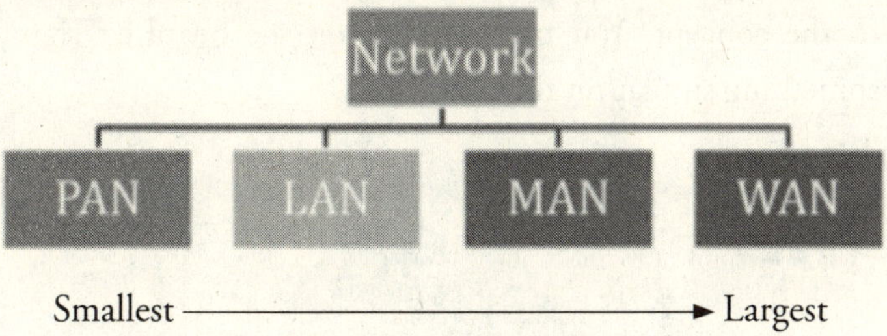

Please share a mind map on the types of networks along with their features before you introduce the fun elements in the class.

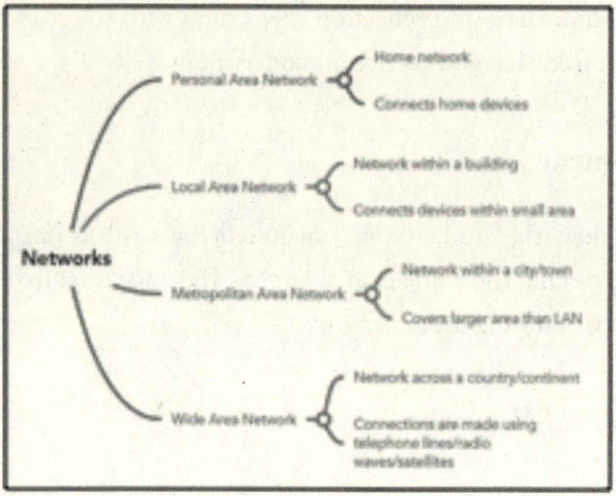

Mind Map on Types of Networks

Internet

A visual impression of the internet will give more clarity to the concept. You may draw it on the board or show something similar on the projector.

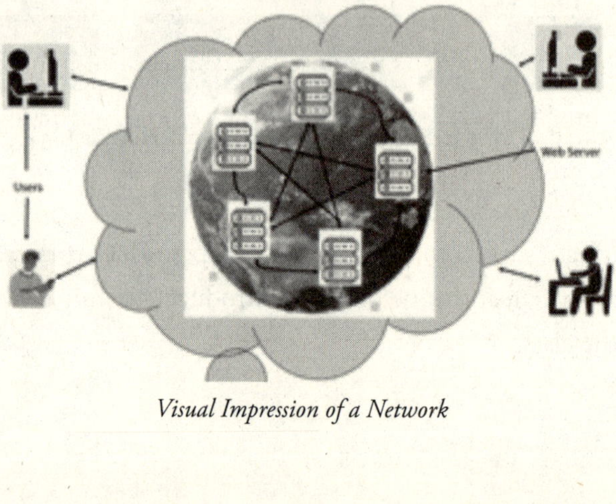

Visual Impression of a Network

Difference Between Internet and Intranet

You may display the images of internet and that of intranet next to each other and prompt the students to find out visible differences. Please give the students cues as and when required.

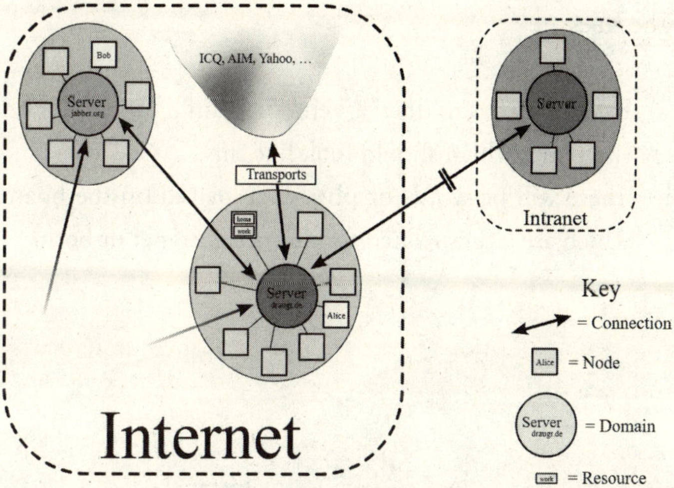

Internet	Intranet
It is a public network. Accessible to all.	Private network. Accessible to members.
Not secure.	Secure.
Most of the content on the web is accessible.	Restricted access to net is available.

Game Time – Venn it Out!

This game is to make the students identify features of internet, intranet and the features which are common to both using a Venn diagram. Divide the class in small groups of three to four students. Please give each group a couple of A4-sized sheets and share the rules of the game with them. The rules are:

a) Each team has to draw a Venn diagram on the given A4 size paper which should look like this.
b) There will be words or phrases displayed on the board which are either related to internet, intranet or both.

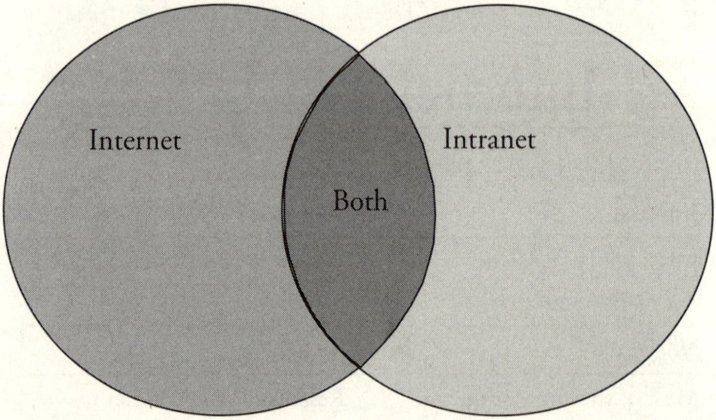

c) The teams need to put the number of each word or phrase in the sections marked internet, intranet and both as will be appropriate.

d) 1 point per correct placement.

The probable clues are shared below, categorized under the heads – **internet only**, **intranet only** and **both**. These have to be displayed to the students in a haphazard order during the game.

Internet Only

- Accessible worldwide.
- Requires Internet Service Provider (ISP).
- Used to access public websites.
- Open to anyone with a connection.

Intranet Only

- Accessible only within an organization.
- Requires login credentials.
- Used in offices, schools and businesses.
- Usually protected by a firewall.

Both

- Uses TCP/IP protocols.
- Can be accessed using a web browser.

- Supports sending and receiving data.
- Requires a device like a computer or smartphone.

Websites

You may decide to use an image similar to the one below, which I assembled from www.shutterstock.com to explain to the students that a website is a collection of webpages created with languages like HTML, CSS, PHP or JavaScript. Websites are stored on remote web servers.

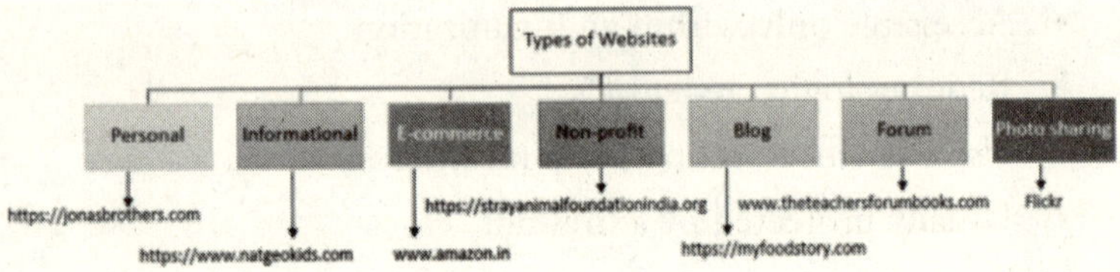

It would be a good idea to share some example Uniform Resource Locators (URLs) of each category, if you decide to use a classification chart like the one above.

You may now decide to discuss the parts of an URL. A couple of samples have been created for you.

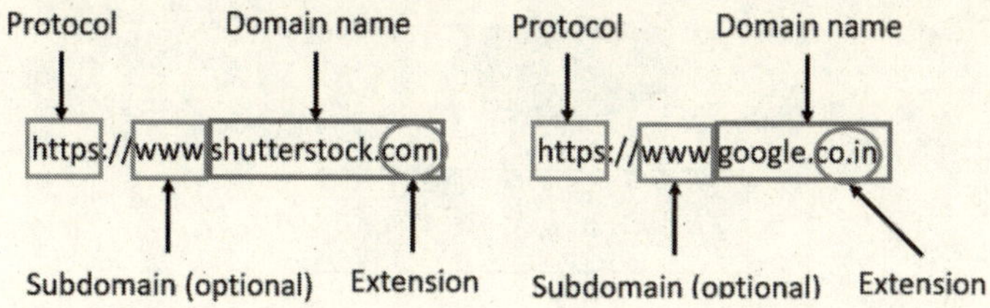

Certain domain name extensions like .com, .org, .edu, .net, .gov and .co are worth mentioning along with some country code extensions.

> You may share this interesting fact that **.ai** which is an official country code extension for Anguilla, a British Overseas Territory is now being used as an extension for websites that are associated with Artificial Intelligence.

Web Browsers

After explaining what web browsers are, it might be a good idea to share a flowchart to explain how a browser works.

Game Time: Spot the Browser!

Please display a random collage of icons from some web browsers and other software as shown below and ask the teams to identify and write down the names of the browsers. The collage below has been created using an AI image generator website which supports text to image conversion.

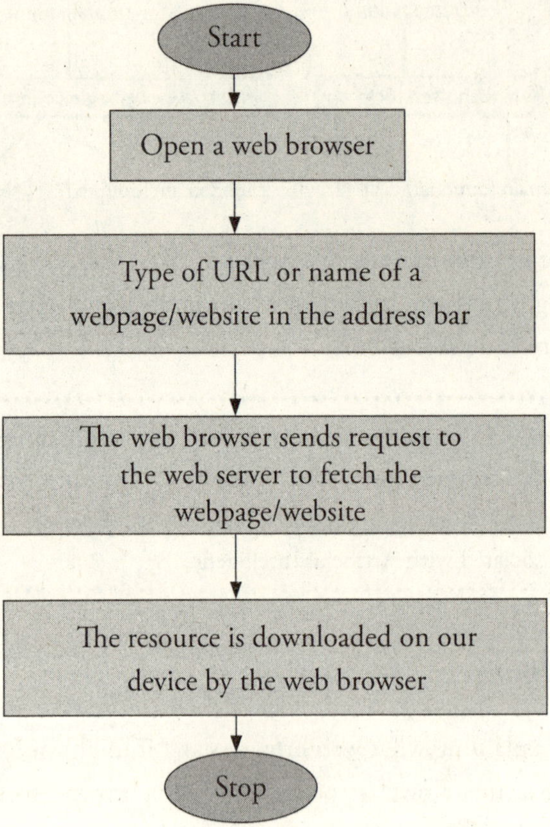

Flowchart on How a Web Browser Works

Give the teams 30 seconds to complete the work. The teams get a point for each browser identified correctly.

The following game is to identify different parts of a browser. Allow the teams 90 seconds to complete the game. One point is to be awarded for each correct answer.

Game Time: Browser Guide

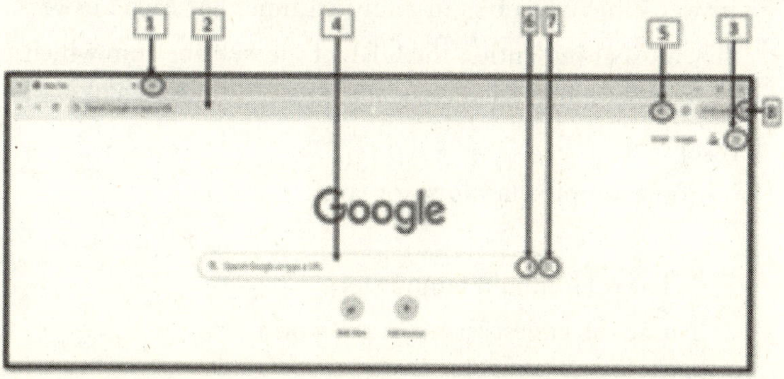

Search Engines

You may begin this section with the following question: what if we do not know the URL of a website?

The students must know the ways they can download a website.

1. **You know the URL** – type the URL in the address bar of the web browser.
2. **You do not know the URL** – type the subject you are looking for in the search bar of a search engine.

Summing Up with a Game

Game Time: Web Scavenging

Note: This game will require the students to use computers and the internet.

The teams need to use a browser and a search engine to answer some questions in a limited time. For each answer, they must also mention the URL of the website from which they have found the answer. Each correct answer will earn two points.

Some sample questions for you.

1. What is Honolulu famous for?
2. Name the largest island in the world.

3. Write the URL of one Government of India website. What is the purpose of the website?
4. Find out the URLs of IIT Kharagpur and IIM Kolkata.
5. Open **kids.nationalgeographic.com** Under the **ANIMALS** tab, go to **AMPHIBIANS** and note the names of any four amphibians.

Suggested Grading Rubric

The following is a suggested rubric to grade the gamified activities you conduct. The best team for each activity will get a badge and the team with the highest score will get an overall badge. Please display the rubric with earned badges on the class display board.

Team Name	Team Members	Venn it Out (12 points)	Spot the Browser (5 points)	Browser Guide (8 points)	Web Scavenging (10 points)	Total Points
Team A						
Team B						
Team C						
Badge		Venn! Genius	Sharp! Shooter	Expert! Guide	Top! Scavenger	Web! Gyani

Home Assignment

Ask the students to create a crossword puzzle using https://puzzlemaker.discoveryeducation.com/, which will contain at least 10 words they learnt on networking and the internet in the class.

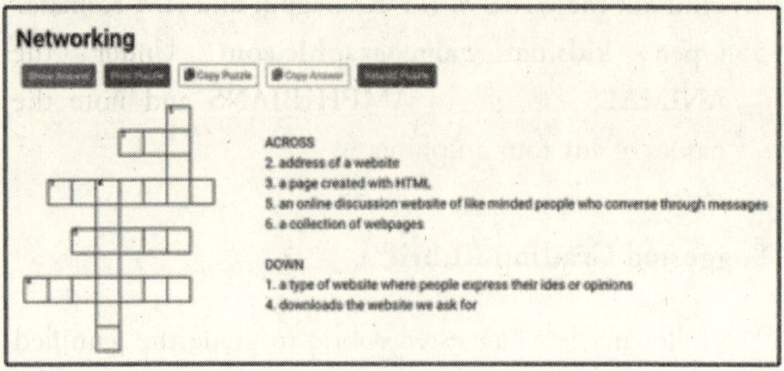

Snapshot of a crossword puzzle created with https://puzzlemaker.discoveryeducation.com/

Creating Email ID Through Experiential Learning, Game-Based Learning and Constructivism

We are going to use a microlearning video and treasure hunting game to learn email ID creation and uses. Most of the students may already have their email IDs; however, creating an ID with a specific purpose makes it more meaningful and interesting.

Topic: Email Creation and Use

Tools used: Microlearning video, treasure hunting game.

Skills: Technology literacy, critical thinking, creativity, communication, questioning, collaboration.

Teaching pedagogy/strategy: Visual and experiential learning.

To make email ID creation interesting and engaging, I have thought of a game which will require the students to take up the role of event organizers. You may decide to use some other strategy if you want.

Problem statement: Assume that the students of the class have confided in you that they want to celebrate Mother's Day in a special way. You, as their computer teacher, take the opportunity to make them learn email creation in a playful method and make them use their new IDs to organize the event. This way, the students will not only create email IDs but also learn to use them.

Please refer to Annexure 2 for this activity, that presents this problem in the form of a treasure hunt game.

Note: The students must be allowed to create the mail IDs at home since they may need mobile verification.

Milestone 1 is linked to a microlearning video that will introduce the students to some basic tips for email ID creation. I have created this with InVideo AI.

Milestone 2 will guide the students to select a meaningful user ID.

Milestone 3 will share the names of some email providers and will suggest that they choose Gmail. The reasons to choose Gmail will also be shared.

Milestone 4 will inform the students about the data they must keep ready to create an ID.

The email icon will inform the students about the components of the compose window.

Step 1. Divide the class into small groups of three to four students.

Step 2. Each group must create a unique email ID, keeping the purpose of the new ID creation in mind. They need to use the treasure hunt game to follow the steps of creation.

Step 3. Each group will write two emails to the class teacher or you, with a copy to the other groups and you/class teacher in the blind copy.

Subject of Mail 1: One idea to celebrate Mother's Day. The class teacher/you, in turn, will select a few ideas and will reply to all the groups.
Subject of Mail 2: The order of events, along with duration for each event and the participant list.
The class teacher/you will create the final order of events by taking ideas from the mails she received and mail the final details to the students.

Step 4. Draft final mail for the principal. Each group will compose an email and send it to you/the class teacher. The best mail will be sent to the principal.

Subject of the Mail to the Principal: Seeking approval to organize Mothers' Day.

Summing Up Assignment

1. Match the columns:

a) Cc	a) a file sent with an email
b) Signature	b) to send an email to a new recipient
c) Attachment	c) Greeting a recipient
d) Recipient	d) Sending copy of an email to others
e) Salutation	e) Personal details which appears at the end of a mail
f) Forward	f) Receiver of an email

2. State true or false:
   a) Email IDs need to be unique for every individual.
   b) It is not essential to include the recipient's email address while sending an email.
   c) The Bcc option allows you to send an email secretly to a recipient.

3. Identify the following icons of Gmail:

Home Assignment

In a Word document, store the screenshots of the steps you took to create the new email ID. Mail the document as an attachment to your teacher.

Learning to Use Google Drive through Project-Based Learning, Peer Teaching and Constructivism

Students at this level are already aware of some of the features of Google Drive and how to use them. I think the best way to teach them this topic would be to make them play a short puzzle game of decoding and applying the Caesar Cypher technique as an introduction, and then letting them create instructional video tutorials in groups.

> **Caesar Cypher**
>
> It is an encryption technique that is used to shift the alphabets of a text by a shift key. It is believed to have been used by Julius Caesar to transmit military intelligence.
>
> Text: Easy
>
> Shift key: 3
>
> Result: Hdvb

Project-based learning would play a pivotal role as the students learn by doing. Creating a tutorial to teach others (peer teaching) would be an interesting challenge for the students. They would take the responsibility of understanding the concepts thoroughly before implementing them. The project would enhance their retention and communication skills and help the students construct new knowledge (constructivism) during the process of creation.

Topic: Using Google Drive

Please refer to the Annexure 3 for this activity.

Tools used: Research, puzzle game, encryption–decryption.

Skills: Technology literacy, media literacy, visual skills, critical thinking, creativity, communication, collaboration.

Teaching pedagogy/strategy: Active and hands-on learning.

Introduction

Please begin with the features of a Google Drive by asking the students questions on the following features of Google Drive.

1. Store important documents and folders as backup in the cloud.
2. Create documents, spreadsheets, slides and save on the drive.
3. Retrieve, download and share files and folders as and when necessary.
4. Storage capacity is 15 GB.

Please clarify the doubts that some students may have. You may decide to make the students play a short puzzle game to gauge their understanding.

Prerequisites for the Lesson

1. Please retain the same groups that were created for email ID creation. This will save you the task of creating Google accounts all over again.
2. Share in the drives of these groups a Word document with instructions to create the video tutorial.
3. The instructions in the file must be in encrypted format to make the exercise more exciting.

The Scenario for the Game

A malware has encrypted some parts of a document '**Instructions.docx**' that you have shared with the groups on their Google Drives. The groups must first open the file, decode the contents of the document and then start creating the tutorial.

Please inform the students that most of the documents have been encrypted using the **Caesar Cypher** method. The **shift key is three** for this document.

At the end of the lesson, the groups must upload their work to their respective drives and complete it at home and share it with you.

Actual Contents of 'Instructions.docx':

Task: Create a video tutorial to teach Google Drive to your juniors.

Software/apps to use: Google Slides and the snipping tool

The tutorial must include the following points:

1. One slide describing the purpose and features of a Google Drive
2. One slide describing how to access the drive.
3. One slide describing how to upload a file/folder on the drive.
4. One slide describing how to download a file/folder on the drive
5. One slide describing how to share a file/folder.
6. One slide describing how to delete a file.

Contents of 'Instructions.docx' After Encryption:

Task: Create a video tutorial to teach the use of Google Drive to your juniors.

Vriwzduh/dss wr xvh – Jrrjoh Volghv dqg Vqlsslqj wrro

Wkh wxwruldo pxvw lqfoxgh wkh iroorzlqj srlqwv –

1. Sxusrvh dqg ihdwxuhv ri d Jrrjoh Gulyh – 1 volgh
2. Krz wr dffhvv wkh gulyh – 1 volgh

3. Xsordg d iloh/iroghu rq gulyh – 1 volgh
4. Grzqordg d iloh/iroghu rq gulyh – 1 volgh
5. Krz wr vkduh d iloh/iroghu – 1 volgh
6. Krz wr ghohwh d iloh – 1 volgh

You may want the students to present their tutorials in the next class. Grade their creativity and add feedback for further improvement.

Learning App Development Through Project-Based Learning, Modelling–Scaffolding or Differentiation Technique

We have used project-based learning earlier in Section 14.3. However, learning to create and use apps through PBL will require a lot of hand-holding. That is why I teach app development to beginners using both modelling–scaffolding as well as PBL techniques. For the students who are a little ahead and are able to build apps already, I prefer using differentiation so that they learn something new without getting bored.

Topic: App Development

Tools used: App Lab of code.org

Skills: Technology literacy, media literacy, visual skills, critical thinking, creativity, communication, collaboration, research.

Teaching pedagogy/strategy: Active and hands-on learning.

Teaching Using Differentiation

Modelling and Scaffolding for Beginners

For the 'I do' part of modelling–scaffolding, first, I think you would like to spark the curiosity of the students by showing them some already existing apps like WhatsApp, Gpay, Uber and ask them about the purpose of these apps. You would also try to show them the UI of these apps from your phone, if possible; otherwise, you may display screenshots of these apps. You can even call upon the advanced learners to take over the responsibility of explanation. This way, you can keep them engaged in peer teaching.

Time to show them app creation next. After showing the design components of **App Lab**, the students must observe you adding code to the objects to create a simple app. I prefer using **App Lab of code.org** as it is easy to design and code, and has a built-in mobile emulator to check the output. *Earlier, I tried MIT App Inventor but found that it is not meant for a class full of students with varied abilities.*

The 'we do' part of the modelling–scaffolding technique must be conducted in the lab. The beginners need to follow you and emulate your actions while you create an app from scratch. *I usually allow the more confident ones to work alone, whereas the ones who want a partner, I allow them to work in pairs.*

For the 'you do' part, I usually ask the students to create a three-screen informative app on any three important landmarks of India. They must use buttons for navigation and labels to write information. They may research the content on the web.

Differentiation for Advanced Learners

The advanced learners can create a quiz app with a scoreboard or a music generation app. Although you will be engaged with the beginners, it would be necessary to take a look at the progress of the advanced learners. They may require your help. If possible, allow them to use the software they are conversant with.

Experiential Learning and Direct Instruction Technique in Action

Role-play is a great way to implement **experiential learning, social learning** as well as **constructivism**. This method teaches learning by doing, learning from observing peers, as well as learning through experience, exploration and interaction. Role-play helps in improving skills like social interaction, verbal communication as well as kinaesthetic skills. In this section, we will use role-play to teach e-commerce as it will help the students to reflect and apply their knowledge earned by doing it practically.

Topic: E-commerce

Tools used: Role-play.

Skills: Technological literacy, media literacy, critical thinking, creativity, communication, collaboration.

Teaching pedagogy/strategy: Active learning.

Introduction

E-commerce

Please introduce the concept of e-commerce by displaying the following diagram or something similar to the students

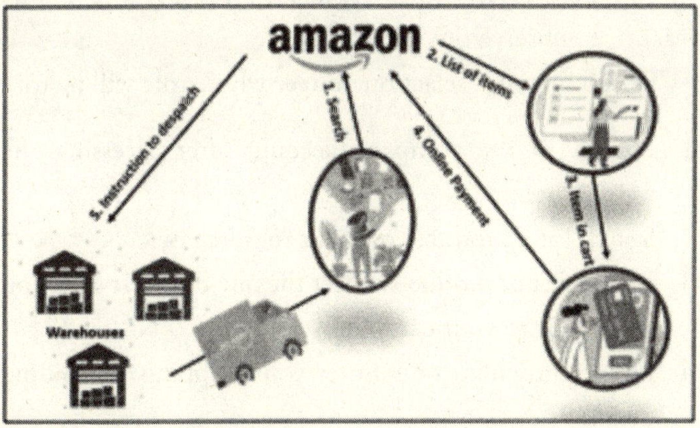

and ask them to identify the steps that are taking place during an online purchase. Add points that they missed.

Role-Play

Please let the students know that they are going to perform role-play to explain their understanding of how e-commerce works.

Divide the class into four to five groups, approximately five to six students per group. Assign each group an e-commerce company, such as Flipkart (electronics, books), Myntra (clothes, shoes), Nykaa (cosmetics), Amazon (electronics, clothes, shoes, cosmetics). Give the groups five to seven minutes to prepare themselves to enact the steps as displayed through the earlier diagram to buy/sell a product. Tell the groups that they will get two minutes to present their role play.

You may invite other teachers, especially the drama teacher, to observe the role play.

For each group, select one **buyer** whose role will be to:

1. Log in to the company account after accessing the website or app.
2. Search for a product you want to purchase.
3. From a list of products, select the one that best suits you and add it to your cart.
4. Proceed to check out. Enter your shipping and billing details.

5. Click on the confirmation button and complete placing your order.

The rest of the students in the group will represent the **back-end system**. Although it is a completely automated process, however, enacting the part of the system will bring clarity to the students. The role of the students representing the **backend system** will be to:

1. **Order Receipt:** A student will receive the order details of the buyer from the online store.
2. **Order Verification:** A student will be responsible for verifying the order, checking whether the product is available, confirming the price and verifying payment.
3. **Payment Processing:** A student will process the payment, check whether the required amount has been paid and generate an order confirmation.
4. **Inventory Management:** A student will be responsible to allocate the ordered items and update inventory(stock) levels.
5. **Fulfilment:** The student will be responsible to organize picking, packing and shipping the order.
6. **Shipping and Delivery:** The student will generate shipping labels, track the shipment, provide delivery status updates to the client and track the order until it is delivered.

Inform the students, although the whole process takes place online within a minute or so, in class, each student will have to enact their role through dialogues. For example, the buyer may say, 'I want a bottle of shampoo.' Instruct them to frame dialogues so that the process of e-commerce is very clear to everybody.

At the end of each presentation, appreciate their efforts first and then point out the areas they missed or could have improved.

GRADING RUBRIC FOR THE TEACHER

Suggested grades	Suggested Grading Pointers
A*	3 Demonstrates excellent understanding of the topic 4 Applied critical thinking and creativity in the script
A	3 Demonstrates good understanding of the topic 4 Tried to apply some critical thinking and creativity in the script
B*	3 Understands the topic 4 Has been able to express 50 per cent of their understanding through role-play
B	3 Has little or no understanding of the topic 4 Had difficulty expressing the concept through role-play

Inquiry-Based Learning and Direct Instruction Technique in Action

Direct Instruction Technique is a structured and straightforward teacher-led instructional approach which we always use to teach a specific concept. We will use **yes/no questions** as a part of the **Direct Instruction Technique** to gauge the understanding of the students.

I usually ask the students to raise their hands for 'yes'. This helps me control the noise level in the class.

We will also use a survey-based project as a part of Inquiry-based learning. Inquiry-based learning allows learners to ask questions, find solutions to problems or scenarios, to come to their understanding.

I have seen that students learn better when they are allowed to explore for answers. Most of my survey-based project initiatives ended with analysing and interpreting data by using spreadsheets. This gives me a dual benefit of letting the students learn the topic at hand on their own and also explore various features of a spreadsheet for modelling real-life data.

Topic: Online Payment

Tools used: Survey-based project, yes/no questions.

Skills: Technology literacy, media literacy, critical thinking, creativity, communication, collaboration.

Teaching pedagogy/strategy: Active learning.

Introduction

E-card

Most of the students must be aware of what e-cards are. You may give them some examples first to make them connect to the concept. Then you may ask yes/no questions to help them consolidate their learning. Some example questions of yes/no questions for you:

1. Are e-cards designed on paper?
2. Can you choose an e-card from a website and send it to your friend on his birthday?
3. Does your friend get a link in his email for the e-card you sent?
4. Can you personalize an e-card?
5. Can you design your e-card on the web?

Online Payment

Please ask the students whether they know what the different ways are to make payments online. Students may have some ideas about the topic; please build on their ideas.

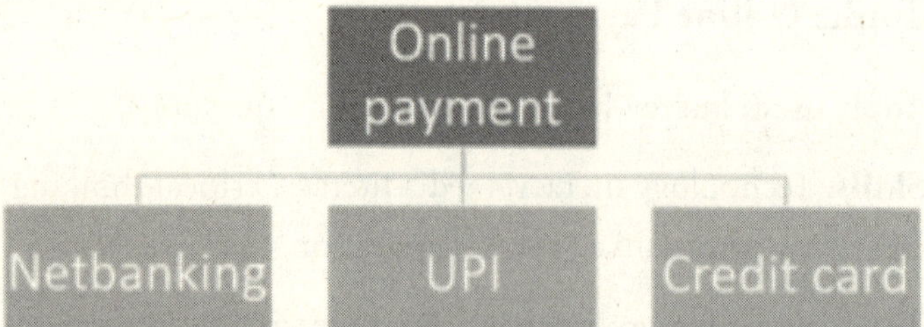

Net banking	UPI	Credit Card
Can be done from any smart device with internet connection.	Unified Payments Interface is a real time payment method which can be done through a mobile app.	Money is taken on credit from a bank whose credit card you hold.
Transaction can be done from the account you hold with a bank.	Multiple bank accounts can be linked to a single app and any one account may be used for payment.	The credit card details like card number, expiry date, card holder name and CVV need to be entered during online payment.
Money is deducted from your bank.	Money is deducted from your bank.	You need to repay the bank after a specific period.

After a brief introduction to the types of online payment, you may create four to five groups in the class.

Their tasks would be:

- To collect survey data from people known to them.
- Each student must collect from at least 25 respondents.
- They may use Google Forms or paper-based forms for data collection.

- The daily data they collect has to be filled into a Google sheet meant for that group. Every student in the group must have access to the sheet.
- They may take four to five days to collect data and two more days to organize the data in the sheet.

The columns in the form may be as follows:

Gender	Age group	Preferred Method of Online Payment	Benefit of Online Payment	Purpose of Online Transaction	Frequency of Transactions	Any Concerns with Online Transaction
Male/ Female	>50 35-50 18-35 <18	1. Credit card 2. Debit card 3. UPI 4. Mobile wallet 5. Cash on delivery 6. No online transactions	1. Fast and convenient 2. Cashless 3. Discounts & offers 4. Others	1. Shopping 2. Food order 3. Transport 4. Bill payment 5. Recharge Others	1. Daily 2. Weekly 3. Monthly 4. No fixed interval	1. Data privacy 2. Fraud 3. Money deducted before placing order

After the data is collected in the Google Sheets, you can give them ideas to analyse and interpret data based on different criteria. A class presentation may be a good idea to grade the students' effort.

Conclusion

You may decide to end the topic with a short debate on '**Social Media Negatively Affects Young Minds**'.

Home Assignment

1. Complete the table below. If you have collected information from the internet, mention the URLs of the websites as sources.

Social Media Sites	
Advantages	**Disadvantages**
1.	1.
2.	2.
3.	3.

2. A toll booth on a highway has five channels to let the vehicles pass. Let us consider each car to be data. Answer the following questions:
   i. What is the bandwidth of the toll booth?
   ii. During office hours, the traffic (data) load at the toll booth is high, which leads to congestion. Suggest

a remedy to this problem using your concept of bandwidth.

Run a speed test on your laptop. Take a screenshot of the upload/download speed and share it in Google Classroom. Before running the speed test, check this video: https://www.youtube.com/watch?v=pefuqiGF98Y

How to Check Internet Speed in Laptop by Tech Related Tips.

Reciprocal Questioning in Action

Reciprocal questioning is a student-centered learning strategy where students and teachers (or students among themselves) take turns asking and answering questions to promote deeper understanding of a topic.

Anthony V. Manzo and Ula C. Manzo introduced **Reciprocal Questioning** strategy in 1969. Their objective was to create a learning process where the teachers and the students learn texts through questioning each other.

It is a dialogue-based strategy in which students and/or teachers take turns generating questions and discussing answers, encouraging active thinking, comprehension and critical inquiry.

Since the topic has been covered in earlier classes, it would be a good idea to implement this strategy to learn file management.

Topics – File Management, Wild Card Characters ('?', '*'), File Formats

Tools to be used:

Hangman and other games, topic related video, reciprocal questioning.

Skills:

Technology literacy, critical thinking, creativity, communication, research and organization skill.

Teaching pedagogy/strategy: Video-based learning, active learning.

Introduction

The topic may be introduced with a video on file management. I found this highly informative video, quite suitable for the middle school students on file management that will help in reinforcing the prior knowledge of the students. Scan the QR code below for the same.

Please let the students know that they will be questioned on the contents of the video. During the video presentation,

Computer Skills Course:
File Management, Part 1

they must take notes and jot down questions on **fuzzy points** for the concepts covered in the video.

Reciprocal Questioning Session

This section may begin with reciprocal questioning (***refer to Chapter 13 on Computer Ethics***). Please display the following images and ask related question(s). Add/modify images and questions as you dim fit. Allow the students to ask you questions intermittently on fuzzy points or on relevant topics.

What do the drawers signify if we compare the chest of drawers with a computer hard disk?

As you can see in the adjacent image that the folders have name tags. Why is it necessary to name files and folders?

C:\Desktop\schooltrip\itinerary.docx

1. What does **C:** stand for?
2. What is **Desktop**?
3. What is **schooltrip**?
4. What is **itinerary docx**?
5. Which part of **itinerary.docx** is the **file name** and which is the **extension?**

The adjacent icon depicts image files.
Can you name an image file extension that stores images of high quality but takes more memory space?
Can you name an image file extension that stores compressed images?

Recall Game on Parts of a File Name

You may play a short recall game based on the video they watched. Draw a table on the board as below and ask the students to call out file extensions they remember from that category.

Documents	Images	Videos	Audios

Wildcard Challenge Game

After explaining what wildcards are, with ample examples, you may want to check the understanding of the students using the following game.

Display or write on the board a series of file names as below.

cat.txt
cap.txt
car.txt
cup.doc
cab.txt
cut.txt
cartoon.png
cool.txt
c?t.txt
c*.txt

Call out a wildcard pattern like c*t.txt or c??.txt, and ask the students to **circle/underline** all matching files.

Summing Up

By now the students are expected to know a lot about file management. Involve them in a **hangman game** which you must create in advance. Display the game on the white board and ask the students to come up with the answers. You may supply clues, or the game also provides hints. Below is the link for a sample game created by me. The clues are provided for your reference.

*The Hangman Game***

***Though the format of the game refers to the concept of hanging, please note that the intention is only to enhance learning through this popular game. If a teacher feels their students could be too sensitive for this, they can skip this game and use some other format that leads to the same outcome.*

Clues are in Haphazard Order:

File names end with this.

Extension for a PowerPoint file.

Collection of data of a particular type.

Extension to a word file.

You can create your own hangman game using this link.
https://www.hangmanwords.com/create

Home Assignment

1. Your father's laptop has four folders on the desktop – Monthly Expenditure, Office, Personal and Entertainment. In which folder would the following files or folders be stored?
   i. leave_application.docx, ii. school_fees receipt.pdf, iii. kids_party photos folder, iv. best_of_kishore_kumar.mp3
2. Which are the Windows default folders? (Research from **support.microsoft.com**)
3. hy do we usually keep meaningful names to the files and folders?
4. What is the difference between the wildcard sequence ???? and *?

File Management Through Experiential Learning

Introduction

This lesson will have to be conducted in the lab. The students must experience what they have learnt in the earlier lesson through hands-on activities. I have shared some sample exercises for you, which you may consider using.

Please create a folder named **assignments**, ready before the class and save it at a convenient location accessible to the students. The folder must have the following items.

One.jpg file containing images of different types of animals.

One.mp4 file. You may download this video clip, accessible through the QR code.

The Lion King Clip

exercise1.docx file containing instructions and questions for Activity 1.

exercise2.docx file containing instructions and questions for Activity 2.

Activity 1 – Using Multiple Applications

Instructions for the Students:

Open **exercise1.docx** file and answer the questions in it. You may keep the .jpg and the .mp4 files minimized on the taskbar to help you answer the questions.

1. List the animals you see in the **.jpg/.jpeg** file.
2. Watch the **.mp4** file. List the animals you see in the video. You may play the video more than once if required.
3. What is the name of the video clip?
4. Save the file **exercise1.docx** as **<your name>exercise1.docx**.

Activity 2 – Use of Wild Card Characters in File Search and Transferring a Folder to Another Drive

** You are requested to store some files and folders in the students' working directory of all the computers in the lab which will yield results for the searches below.

1. Press **windows key**. In the search box type the required search criteria.
2. List out all the files having names that start with 'a'.
3. List out all the files having names that start with 'a' and end with 't'.

4. List out all the .docx files.
5. List out all the .docx files that have 3 letter file names.
6. List out all the .docx files that have 3 letter file names beginning with 'a' and ending with 't'.
7. Right click on the **assignment** folder; a sliding menu will appear. Select the option **cut**. Double click on **This PC** icon on the desktop or click on the folder icon on the taskbar. A new window will open. You will get to see an icon for **drive D** on the left-hand panel of the window. Double click on it. The drive will open. Right click and choose **paste**. This way you can transfer data from one drive to another or to a pen drive.

Home Assignment

Select a file and a folder from your desktop and copy them to a pen drive. Share a screenshot of the paste operation in Google classroom.

Chapter 15

Applying Constructionism in PBL

PBL (Project Based Learning) is rooted in Constructivism, Experiential Learning, Social Learning Theory as well as Constructionism. The theory of **Constructionism** was pioneered by Seymour Papert, who felt that the students learn best when they build a tangible product – digital, physical, or conceptual, that signifies '**learning by making**'. The theory applies perfectly in tech-related PBL like making presentations, apps, or models.

Applying **Project-Based Learning (PBL)** to teach **Operating Systems (OS)**, **User Interface (UI)** and **Language Translators** makes these concepts realistic, relatable and engaging.

I feel system software and its components can be taught best by **Didactic Teaching** strategy, a teacher-centric instructional strategy where the teacher explains concepts and delivers information verbally using videos, slide deck or a board as aid, the students listen, take notes and absorb content.

Since I love to use PBL at every opportunity I get; for this topic, I prefer using PBL as an end-of-the-chapter activity to enable students to consolidate the concepts. Let me share some challenging project ideas which you may assign applying **Differentiation** or **Multiple Intelligence** technique.

Project Ideas: Design an OS for **either** your **school computers** or for **a mobile device for children**.

Points to Note:

School OS – for classrooms, teachers, students and administrators.

Mobile Device for Children – for educational information, educational games and receiving calls from parents.

Keeping the target group in mind, the students may use any one of the following visual aids to present their ideas.

i. a presentation
ii. an app
iii. a video

They must design and explain the kind of UI they would like to design.

The functions the OS must have.

The kind of security that will be provided.

Additionally, the advanced students may include:

- Voice assistant feature
- AI-based study/game suggestions
- Screen reader for accessibility

Please find below some questions that may be asked to sum up the topics.

1. What type of operating system is Windows?
2. How many main memories are used in a multiprocessor system?
3. Share an example of multitasking by an operating system.
4. Why do you think security is required even for a single user system?
5. Do you think a computer can work without an operating system? Explain.
6. What is the key difference between a multiprocessor and a multiprogramming operating system?
7. What is the similarity between a multiprocessor and a multiprogramming operating system?
8. Imagine you are a network operating system managing 10 computers. Computer1 has requested to print a file, Computer4 has requested to share a file with Computer2 and Computer9 wants to download a file

from the internet. Which functions of an operating system do you think you have to handle?

9. Imagine you are a network operating system managing 10 computers. Computer1 has requested to print a file, Computer4 has requested to share a file with Computer2 and Computer9 wants to download a file from the internet. How would you schedule these jobs for the CPU. Do not search for the answer on the web, I want to check your logic.
10. You should use mobile OS as well as the Windows operating systems. Mention 2 differences and 2 similarities.

Chapter 16

Herbert Spencer's Principle of Correlation and Constructivism

I have seen that while introducing new concepts like network, correlating with other subjects makes learning more relevant and meaningful. Herbert's **Horizontal Correlation** means linking a topic in one subject with related topics in other subjects, so students can see how one subject is interconnected with other subjects. Correlation helps with improved retention, problem solving and critical thinking skills among students.

Although **Direct Instruction Technique** is necessary to teach the topic network thoroughly, I prefer using case study-based questionnaire at the end to gauge the understanding of the students.

> Herbert Spencer first conceived the idea of correlating the teaching of various subjects. 'All knowledge is one unit'.

Horizontal Correlation and Problem-Based Learning in Action

In this lesson, I will share with you how I implement Horizontal Correlation to introduce the topic network. I will also share a few case studies along with relevant questions that may be used as end-of-the-chapter exercise. It would be better to assign each case study to a group of 3–4 students, so that they can discuss and answer the questions.

Topic – Network

Tools to be used: Topic related video, correlation with biology, visualization.

Teaching pedagogy/strategy: Herbert's theory of correlation – horizontal correlation, visual learning, visualization.

Introduction

In this lesson, we will try to implement **horizontal/external correlation**, which means correlating the concept of one subject with another. The following **Spider Map** shows the subject-wise correlation with Computer Network.

You may begin the lesson by displaying a similar spider map and drawing a correlation between any subject you are comfortable with and computer network. I usually correlate between **Central Nervous System** (**CNS**) of human body and computer network. There are quite a few similarities between the two. You may show the following video of

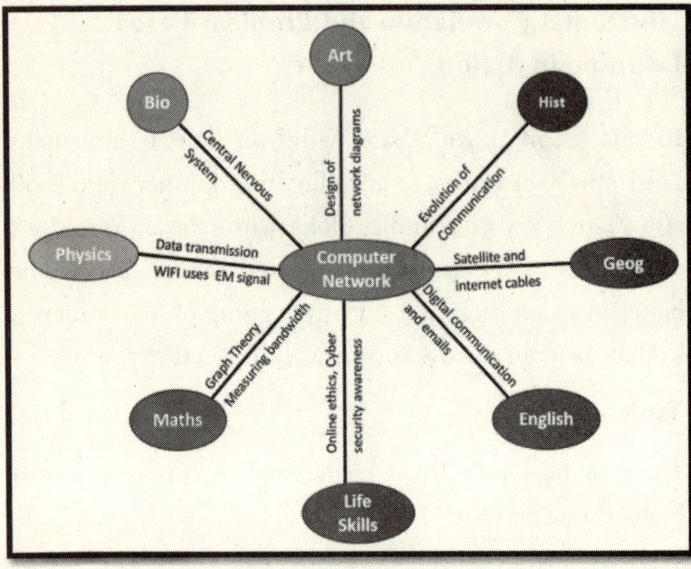

The Central Nervous System

central nervous system that the students will be able to relate with.

After the subject-wise correlation through Spider Map, you may display the following diagram or something similar and explain the computer network. Then go on to point out the similarities between the CNS and the computer network using the comparison table shared below or a video created on the same theme using invideo.ai. Here is the QR code for the video.

CNS vs Computer Network – A Fascinating Correlation

While planning this topic please consult with the biology teacher to ensure that the information you are about to share

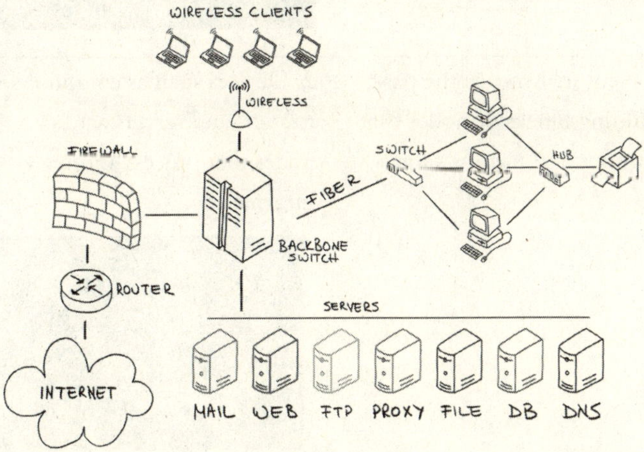

with the class is correct in all respects. Please do not get into the details of the nervous system as that will create confusion and will be a waste of time. You may use images like the ones used here to help students visualize the similarities.

Similarities between CNS and Computer Network**	
Central Nervous System (CNS)	**Computer Network**
1. Information is transmitted through neurons via electrical impulses and chemical signals across synapses. 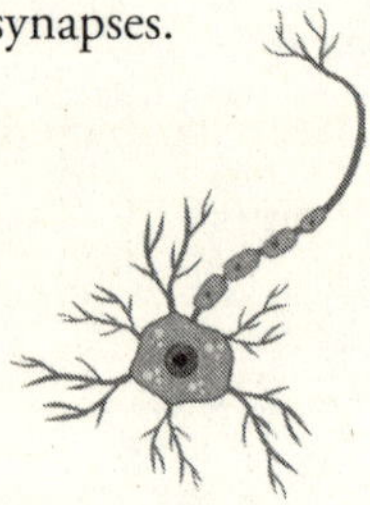	1. Data is transmitted through cables, wireless signals, or optical fibers. 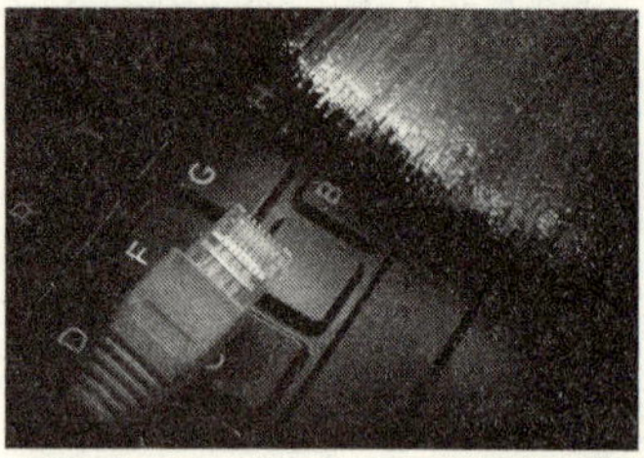
2. Neurons serve as the basic building blocks or nodes that transmit and process signals.	2. Devices such as computers, routers, and servers act as nodes that process and relay information. 

3. The brain serves as the central control center, regulating and coordinating various bodily functions and responses. 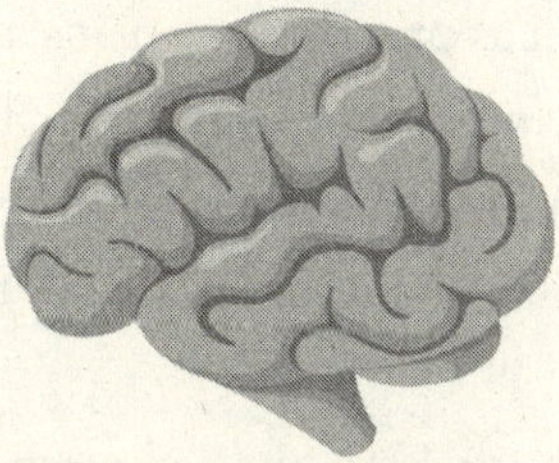	3. A server or a central processing unit (CPU) serves as the control center, manages and coordinates network activities.

**** The points of similarities have been collected from chatgpt.com.**

Formative Assessment Through Case Studies

I have shared a few case studies which you may use in class to assess the students' understanding.

Case Study 1 for LAN

At ABC School, the managing committee and the principal have decided to upgrade IT infrastructure to enable the students and the teachers to work more efficiently. The school has planned to install 20 new desktop computers in the computer lab. The library and staff room will also receive computers and a printer each. All the systems will be connected to one another using network cables and switches.

Now, the students will be able to print their projects from any computer in the lab. Teachers in the staff room will be able to access student records stored on a central server in the computer lab as well as print lessons plans and question papers from the only printer in the staff room. The internet connection is shared among all computers, and the library database will now be available on every device in the school building.

All these computers are located within the same school building and are not connected to any other schools or outside networks, except through a single shared internet connection.

Read the case study carefully and answer the questions that follow.

i. Which type of network do you think is being set up in the school? Justify your answer.
ii. What benefits (any two) do you think the teachers and the students will be getting from this network?
iii. What benefits do you think the school management will get by installing this infrastructure?

Case Study 2 for MAN

ABC group owns a school, a factory, a hospital as well as a college in a city within a radius of 45 kilometers. Each of these facilities has their own LAN. The director of ABC group wants to get information from all these facilities sitting at his office at the head quarter. He also wants to enable communication and data sharing between all the facilities through this network. For the purpose of data security, he wants this to be a private network. To make this a reality, he has hired you. You need to give him suggestions on the following:

i. The type of network. Your justifications for the same.
ii. The medium of communication you would like to use.
iii. Draw a sketch for your proposed network.

Case Study 3 for WAN

GlobalTech Solutions is a multinational company with offices in India, Germany, the United States and Japan. Each office has its own internal network (LAN), where employees can share files, access printers and use local databases.

- To ensure smooth operations across all branches, GlobalTech has a global network that allows:
- The head office in New York can access employee records from all branches.
- Employees from different branches can perform video calls, share documents and use cloud services in real-time.

- Software updates and business data can be shared instantly across continents.
- Employees can log into the central company portal from any office worldwide.

This entire system uses leased communication lines, undersea fiber-optic cables and satellite links to stay connected 24/7. All offices are thousands of kilometers apart, but they work together as if they were in one building.

i. Which type of network is being used by GlobalTech?
ii. Give reasons for your answer.
iii. Why is this network necessary for a company like GlobalTech?

Case Study 4 for CAN

XYZ International School has four main buildings:

- The administrative building
- The main academic building
- The science, music, drama, robotics and computer labs
- The library and the auditorium

Each building has its own network that connects computers, printers, projectors and the servers. To enable communication and resource sharing across the buildings, the school's IT team has connected all the buildings using fiber-optic cables laid underground within the campus boundary.

Now:

- The student data is accessible from any building.
- Students can print their files stored in the server of the computer lab even from the library.
- The school's central server has School Management System software installed. This allows the office to record attendance of staff, the teachers can manage performance appraisal of the students and the principal's office can send circulars and notices across all departments.

This new network allows everyone to be digitally connected within the boundaries of the school.

i. Which type of network is being used by the school?
ii. Give reasons for your answer.
iii. Why is this network necessary for the school?

Summing Up

Please find below a few critical thinking questions which you may use at the end of the lesson to assess the progress of the students.

Some critical thinking questions:

At the end of the lesson, you may ask students to answer the following questions and may add your own as well. Instead of letting them write, it will be wise to ask them because at this point in time their concepts may not have formed properly.

1. The computer lab of a school has 20 computers but only 2 printers. How do you think the students take printouts for their projects even though no printer is attached to their computers? How do you think this system benefits the school?
2. Connecting your Bluetooth headphones to your mobile phone for listening to songs is an example of Personal Area Network. Share another example of PAN.
3. Suggest situations where a school will use either LAN, CAN or WAN.
4. What can be the probable medium of communication in the following situations:
    - i. Two devices in two different rooms of a house.
    - ii. You have a laptop and a smart phone in a room with no network or Wi-Fi, and you are trying to connect to the internet from the laptop.
    - iii. You are trying to connect all the smart devices in your house like TV, mobile phones, tablets and iPod to internet.

iv. A school has 5 branches in a city. What could be the probable medium of communication within each branch? What could be the probable medium of communication between branches?

Home Assignment

Please prepare a glossary of the following terms and share with the students. The students must learn the terms from the resources you share and also from the web if they want extra reading. The terms are – meaning of various terms related to internet: Intranet, URL, ISP, IP address, DNS, webpage, website, web portal, MODEM, switch, hub, router, gateways, link, hyperlink, hypertext, bandwidth. Purpose of the protocols HTTP, FTP, TCP/IP, IMAP, SMTP.

Please inform your students that the next class will be a flipped classroom or they may have to do role play/JAM.

Flipped Classroom and JAM in Action

For this topic, we are going to use the Flipped Classroom concept in a slightly different way. As you have seen in chapter 15, we have asked students to come prepared for this lesson with terms related to internet. Instead of making them teach in the class, we will make them participate in JAM (Just A Minute).

JAM is a learning strategy that promotes **Cognitive Learning** and **Experiential Learning** by making the students participate in short oral activities that improves the students' alertness, focus, communication skill and tests their understanding through the way they apply their knowledge of previously learned concepts.

I have also designed a maze game for the students to make them understand the concept of **Packet Switching** for data transmission. I hope you will find this game relevant for the class.

Topic – Terms Related to the Internet

Tools to be used: Games, flipped classroom, JAM (Just A Minute).

Skills: Technology literacy, critical thinking, creativity, communication, research and organization skills.

Teaching pedagogy/strategy: Blended learning, game-based learning, collaborative teaching.

Lesson Preparation

Before the lesson, refer to Annexure I and photocopy the **TCP-IP maze game** or you may create something on your own. Provide each student with a **photocopy** and **one piece of thick thread** to measure the length of communication paths in the maze. The game is self-explanatory; however, it might be a good idea to call out the rules of the game.

For the JAM, have a **bowl of chits** ready. On each chit, write one topic out of the 22 odd topics you shared as **internet glossary** and the topics taught in the pervious lesson. If you have more students, repeat a few topics or add some extra.

Please request the teacher of the next lesson to spare 5 minutes of her lesson if you overshoot time.

Introduction (2 minutes)

Please inform the students that this lesson will be dedicated to a **maze game** and **JAM**. Explain the rules of JAM. The bowl of chit needs to be passed to each student. The student has to pick up a chit and start speaking immediately for a maximum of **one minute**. Allow the students to use chalkboard if they would like to explain something but they cannot exceed time. To minimize the gap between the presentation of two students, allow the next student to pick up a chit just before the earlier one finishes. If anyone has a question, he/she needs to note it down and ask at the end of all presentations, during the Q&A round. As a moderator, your task will be to oversee smooth execution of JAM, keep time (use stopwatch from your mobile) and conduct the Q&A session.

Maze Game (5 minutes)

Pair up the students, so that they may discuss while playing. The students must finish answering on the sheets you provided. Collect the sheets at the end of the game.

JAM (25–27 minutes)

Please invite one of the colleagues from your department to mark or grade the activity as you will be busy in moderation. A suggested grading rubric is shared below.

TEACHER'S GRADING RUBRIC FOR JAM

Grade	Marks (FM-10)	Suggested grading pointers
A*	9-10	1. Demonstrated excellent understanding of the topic. 2. Applied critical thinking and creativity. 3. Satisfactorily answered the audience question.
A	7-8	1. Demonstrated a good understanding of the topic. 2. Tried to apply some critical thinking and creativity. 3. Partially answered audience question.
B*	5-6	1. Understands the topic. 2. Partially explained the concept. 3. Could not answer the audience question.
B	3-4	1. Has little or no understanding of the topic. 2. Had difficulty framing his answer. 3. Could not answer audience question.

Summing Up (5 minutes)

Please invite your colleague to share feedback on your students' understanding and performance. Request him/her to rectify any misconceptions the students may have through explanations.

Active Learning and Debates in Action

Cloud computing is a topic of interest for students. You will be amazed to see how well informed they are. Instead of teaching them the concept, you may decide to give them the opportunity to come prepared with pre-class materials which you may share online as well as from their textbooks.

Class debates allow the students to actively participate in critical thinking and collaboration to formulate arguments based on prior read as well as evidence and statistics.

Topic: Cloud Computing

Tools to be used: In-class debate.

Skills: Technology literacy, critical thinking, creativity, communication, leadership, research and collaborative learning skills.

Teaching pedagogy/strategy: Blended learning, cross-curricular learning.

Prior Preparation (Must Be Completed a Week Prior to the Event)

Please instruct the students to go through the comic strip which introduces the concept of cloud computing from an e-book containing interesting comic strips on different topics. The name of the book is **Computer Science grade 8 Mel and Conji** by UoLo available at https://issuu.com/tekie-app/docs/cbse_g8_e-book_lr. A QR code is shared below to access the same.

Comic Strip on Cloud Computing

I found this book interesting, makes self-learning quite simple. The students must be informed that they may do additional research if they like and be prepared to participate in an in-class debate. The topic of the debate could be – '**The benefits of cloud computing outweigh its risks**' or '**Schools should store student data on the cloud**'.

It will depend on the size of the class whether you will need two sessions or just one. I would like all my students to take part.

If you require two sessions, divide the class into two groups. Group 1 will participate in the debate in one session and Group 2 in another session. This way you will be able to involve all the students in the class. Select two students from each group who will moderate the debates. Please send them to their English teacher for guidance. The speakers for and against the motion may be decided by a draw of chits. **The moderators as well as the speakers will have to be marked for their performance**.

Invite at least one computer teacher and an english teacher to judge the debate on both the days. You may invite other teachers to be in the audience. **Please arrange for an hour each to conduct the debates**.

The debate

There are plenty of grading rubrics available online for debates. This one caught my eyes –

Grading Rubric Sample

Suggested grading rubric for the moderators can be accessed through the QR code below.

Grading Rubric for moderators

Please take help of the English teacher to modify the grading rubrics according to your requirements. You may use these grades or marks for formative assessment.

Chapter 17

Applying Experiential Learning in Lab Activities

While teaching MS Word, Excel or PowerPoint we tend to focus more on teaching the sub-topics rather than looking at the bigger picture. We set up assignments keeping only the sub-topic in focus. The purpose of having these applications in the syllabus is to make the students appreciate how these applications can be used in our daily lives. To do that, we need to set up assignments carefully, keeping not only the topic at hand but also all the other topics they have learnt earlier.

I have received good results by letting students start working directly on an assignment instead of giving them any demo. What I do is keep a tutorial for the topic ready and saved on the desktop of each computer in the lab, so that, if the students are stuck, they could refer to the tutorial while completing the assignment.

I am sharing some examples of the kind of assignments I have seen the students take interest in.

MS PowerPoint, navigation buttons

I usually ask the students to create a story board on paper or their exercise books with the all the slides they would like to create for their presentation. For example, to create a quiz on PPT they would need two slides for "correct answer" and "wrong answer" for every slide with questions. The story board must look like a slide sorter with links connecting the slides. I have noticed that the students make less mistakes in linking slides if they create a storyboard like this. Of course, they do not like it initially, but get accustomed to after they find its utility. Please find below a sample story board for a quiz presentation.

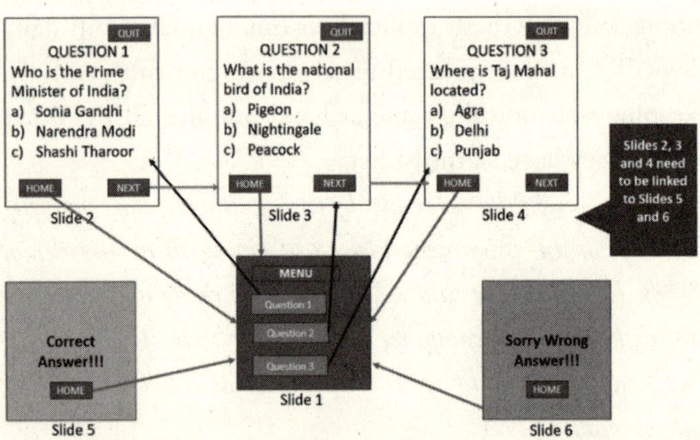

The story board along with a check list will help the students ensure that the links have been done correctly.

Checklist for Links

- ☐ Question 1 button to Slide 2
- ☐ Question 2 button to Slide 3
- ☐ Question 3 button to Slide 4
- ☐ Slide 2 Home button to Slide 1
- ☐ Slide 3 Home button to Slide 1
- ☐ Slide 4 Home button to Slide 1
- ☐ Slide 2 Next button to Slide 3
- ☐ Slide 3 Next button to Slide 4
- ☐ Quit buttons to stop
- ☐ Slide 2 Next button to Slide 3
- ☐ Option b button of Slide 2 to Slide 5

MS Word, tables and columns

Apart from timetable making, holiday list etc. I make it a point to engage the students in creating **comic strips** using table. The students get thrilled to create such comic strips. It not only enhances their command over table handling, gives them a scope to use their creativity. I allow the students download images of comic characters they want; some prefer creating their own characters using MS Paint. Using callouts many of them create wonderful comic strips.

I ask the students to create restaurant menu, recipe booklet or class news using **columns**. Usually these are group projects of 2-3 students. Each student is responsible to collect information for the booklet and also the layout and design. At the last page, I ask them to write down in a text box, information collection on, say for example, pizza, done by, the name of the student. They also mention which page has been designed by whom.

MS Excel, projects

You have seen in earlier chapters that I am fond of making the students conduct survey and then analyse the data using Excel. Let me share an example, I may make the students collect data on the type of newspapers used at home. Each student must collect at least 25 records. At the end of data collection, I allow a group of 4 students to exchange their data, so that each student gets a dataset of 100. Apart from data analysis with charts, I specify the font styles for header, sub-header, font colour, cell colour, type of border etc. so that the students perform formatting too while doing the analysis. At the end, I ask them to **link** the worksheet to a word document where they write their interpretation. Another very important thing for data collection is the format they use to collect data. This aspect displays their critical thinking and creative skills. Before marking the projects, I collect the data collection forms to mark them on that aspect.

We all know that programming is not a cup of tea for all the students in the class. Many students drop the subject after grade 8. In order to popularise the subject, you may use **Differentiation** in class while selecting problems for the students. I make it a point to keep three sets of problems for – the ones struggling, intermediate learners and advanced learners. This way, the ones who take more time to learn coding gets a breather. The intermediate and the advanced learners are challenged according to their capabilities. Everyone in the class remain engaged fruitfully.

I have received a lot of positive response by following **Kolb's Experiential Cycle** while teaching practical topics.

1. **Concrete Experience** – I let them do the lab activity either with me or on their own.
2. **Reflective Observation** – During every project or major assignment I let them discuss the problems they faced while doing the project.
3. **Abstract Conceptualization** – Let them connect their experience to theory in order to overcome their problems.
4. **Active Experimentation** – Try alternative methods to overcome problem.

We have come to the end of this book. Hope I have been able to deliver something new which you can experiment with. Sometimes we get so bogged down because of the syllabus, we forget to introduce the element of fun in learning. It is possible to make our lessons fun even within the strict time schedule. What we need to do is **Ideate and Plan**…

ANNEXURES

Annexure I

A Case Study on ILOVEYOU Virus

The ILOVEYOU virus, also known as the Love Bug or Loveletter, was a VBScript computer worm that spread rapidly in May 2000, infecting millions of Windows computers worldwide. It was transmitted via email, with the subject line 'ILOVEYOU' and an attachment disguised as a love letter.

How it spread:

- The virus was designed to be a self-replicating worm, meaning it didn't need user interaction to spread after it was activated.
- It exploited vulnerabilities in Microsoft Outlook and Windows, allowing it to replicate itself without needing user interaction.

- When a user opened the infected email attachment, the virus would send copies of itself to everyone in the user's address book.
- This rapid spread caused widespread chaos and disruption, especially in government agencies and large corporations.

Impact:

- The ILOVEYOU virus caused significant economic damage, estimated at $3 billion to $15 billion, primarily due to labour costs for cleanup and recovery efforts.
- Its widespread impact led to a global reassessment of cybersecurity practices and increased awareness of the dangers of opening email attachments.
- It highlighted the potential dangers of clicking on suspicious links or attachments in emails.

Key points:

- The ILOVEYOU virus was a significant event in computer security history, demonstrating the power of email-borne malware.
- It taught important lessons about the importance of email security practices, such as being cautious about opening attachments from unknown sources.
- It led to increased vigilance and improved security measures to protect against future cyber threats.

Annexure II

TCP-IP Maze Game

Rishita wants to upload her painting to Facebook from her home laptop. This is a broad overview as to how the TCP/IP will help her achieve this.

1. Her laptop will find the IP address of Facebook from DNS.
2. As soon as the IP address is found the TCP starts sending data to the nearest network device, the wi-fi router at Rishita's house.

3. As the file is large the IP protocol will split the file into equal sized packets. P1-P6 in this case.
4. The router transfers the packets via multiple telecommunication channels to another router closer to the destination IP address.
5. The packets may take any route to reach the destination, usually the fastest.
6. If a packet is lost or damaged TCP will resend the packet.
7. The packets may reach the destination in random order. TCP will arrange the packets in order. The actual image will be formed.
8. Facebook will acknowledge the receipt and the image will be displayed.

Instructions to Play the Game

Study the maze of communication channels carefully. The IP protocol has split the painting into 6 equal-sized packets, P1–P6. These packets are lined up to be transmitted to the Facebook IP address via multiple communication lines. The arrows indicate the starting point of the packets journey.

1. You need to trace the path each packet will take. Mark with pen or pencil.
2. Measure the length of the path for each packet using the thread provided.
3. Assuming one inch of path traversed is equivalent to .005 nanoseconds of time, find out the time taken by each packet to reach the destination.
4. Which packets took the shortest and the longest time?
5. Calculate the total time taken to upload the image on Facebook.
6. The packets have reached the destination in a haphazard manner. What will TCP do?

Image Copyright Information

Page 2: Time Machine Garuda: Canva.AI

Page 3: Bird's Eye View of Ancient Taxila: Canva.AI

Page 4: Chanakya: Lead UI UX Designer/Shutterstock.com; Chandragupta: Sumit Kherde/Shutterstock.com; Panini: Shutterstock AI Generator/Shutterstock.com; Jivika: sattra yothakhammee/Shutterstock.com

Page 9: The Five Guiding Pillars of NEP: Author generated

Page 10: Four Levels of Learning Standards: Author generated

Page 13: Bloom's Taxonomy: Piscine26/Shutterstock.com

Page 14: Unity Platform: Iljanaresvara Studio/Shutterstock.com

Page 19: VARK Model: Skyline Graphics/Shutterstock.com

Page 20: Blackhat Movie Poster: DatBot / Fair Use / https://en.wikipedia.org/wiki/File:Blackhat_poster.jPage#filelinks

Page 21: The Social Network Movie Poster: Daniel Clark Creative / Fair Use / https://en.wikipedia.org/wiki/The_Social_Network#/media/File:The_Social_Network_film_poster.png

Page 30: Zone of Proximal development: desdemona72/ Shutterstock.com

Page 34: Scaffolding Flow Chart: Author generated

Page 36: Experiential Learning: Skyline Graphics/ Shutterstock.com

Page 38: Maslow's Hierarchy of Needs: Julee Ashmead/ Shutterstock.com

Page 48: Components of a Computer System: Author generated

Page 61: Experiential Learning Cycle: Skyline Graphics/ Shutterstock.com

Page 65: Block Diagram: Author generated

Page 70: Binary Cards: https://classic.csunplugged.org/documents/activities/binary-numbers/unplugged-01-binary_numbers.pdf

Page 74: Mind Map on Number Systems: Author generated

Page 82: Conversion between Different Number Systems: Author generated

Page 92: Simple Mind Map: 22TREE HOUSE/Shutterstock.com; Mind Map Infographic: UniqueDesigner38/ Shutterstock.com

Page 94: Timeline Infographic 1: Elegant Solution/ Shutterstock.com; Timeline Infographic 2: onmyvespa/ Shutterstock.com

Page 95: Types of Computers: bannosuke/Shutterstock.com; Minicomputer: Roman Belogorodov/Shutterstock.

com; Mainframe Computer: Oleksiy Mark/Shutterstock.com; Supercomputer: IM Imagery/Shutterstock.com

Page 98: Features of Smartphones Mind Map: Author generated; Mind Map on Broad Computer Categories: Author generated

Page 99: Sample Timeline: Author generated

Page 103: Created using https://app.story-boards.ai

Page 104: Steps to Make Cup Noodles: Yusak_P/Shutterstock.com

Page 108: Steps to Make a Sandwich: Cucumber: New Africa/Shutterstock.com; Bread: Ermak Oksana/Shutterstock.com; Cheese: New Africa/Shutterstock.com; Lettuce: itor/Shutterstock.com; Sandwich: Nataliya Arzamasova/Shutterstock.com

Page 110: Flowchart for Stages in Software Development: Author generated

Page 111: Calculator and Flowchart: Author generated

Page 113: Flowchart: Author generated

Page 117: Algorithm Chart: Author generated

Page 121: Flowcharts: Author generated

Page 125: Vygotsky's Zone of Proximal Development: Danawan Purbanggoro/Shutterstock.com

Page 128: Flowchart: Author generated

Page 133: Flowchart: Author generated

Page 135: Flowchart: Author generated

Page 142: Types of Malware: Mashkavector/Shutterstock.com

Page 144: Concept Map: Author generated

Page 145: Concept Maps: Author generated

Page 150: Firewall Working: SuriyaPhoto/Shutterstock.com

Page 153: Multiple Intelligences Theory: Celia Bornas/Shutterstock.com

Page 165: Jigsaw Technique: Putukas01, CC BY-SA 4.0 <https://creativecommons.org/licenses/by-sa/4.0>, via Wikimedia Commons

Page 181: Network: Author generated

Page 182: Network Types Mind Map: Author generated; Visual Impression of a Network: John T Takai/Shutterstock.com

Page 183: Internet vs Intranet: XZise, CC BY-SA 3.0 <https://creativecommons.org/licenses/by-sa/3.0>, via Wikimedia Commons

Page 184: Internet and Intranet Venn Diagram: Author generated

Page 186: Web server: AlekseyVanin/Shutterstock.com; Website: Rvector/Shutterstock.com; Webpages: Author generated

Pages 186–87: Chart: Author generated

Page 188: Flowchart: Author generated

Page 189: Browser Guide: Author generated

Page 192: Puzzle: https://puzzlemaker.discoveryeducation.com/

Page 195: Icons: Author generated

Page 203: Ecommerce: Author generated

Page 208: Flowchart: Author generated

Pages 214–215: Reciprocal Questioning: Wooden dresser: Anton Starikov/Shutterstock.com; File folders: Elena Elisseeva/Shutterstock.com; Icon: Anastasia_B/Shutterstock.com

Page 228: Spider Map: Author generated

Page 229: Computer Network: Oez/Shutterstock.com

Pages 230–231: CNS and Computer Network: Neuron cell: Perfect_kebab/Shutterstock.com; Cables and signals: Michal_Jesensky/Shutterstock.com; Wifi and router: ImageFlow/Shutterstock.com; Brain: ViJul/Shutterstock.com; CPU: Aleksandr_Lysenko/Shutterstock.com

Page 241: Blended Learning: TarikVision/Shutterstock.com

Pages 246–247: Storyboard: Author generated

Pages 255–256: Annexure II: TCP-IP Maze Game: Nursery Art Design/Shutterstock.com;